15 Minutes to Build a Stronger Marriage

BOBBIE & MYRON YAGEL

Tyndale House Publishers, Inc.
WHEATON, ILLINOIS

This book is dedicated to

Our adult children: Craig, Stephen, and Wendy,
constant sources of love, joy, and pride;

Our daughter-in-law Denise and son-in-law Jeff,
who fit so beautifully into our family;

Our grandchildren, Amber, Devin, Brandon, and Daniel,
our delights, so easy to adore and cherish.

Introduction   ix
How to Get the Most out of This Book   xiii

LEVEL ONE
Week 1: Love *Speaks*   3
Week 2: Togetherness *Gazes*   7
Week 3: Acceptance *Appreciates*   11
Week 4: Commitment *Wills*   13
Week 5: Communication *Listens*   17
Week 6: Conflict Resolution *Chooses*   21
Week 7: Forgiveness *Touches*   25
Week 8: Emotional Intimacy *Opens Up*   29
Week 9: Physical Intimacy *Strokes*   33
Week 10: Spiritual Life *Blesses*   37

LEVEL TWO
Week 11: Love *Discovers*   43
Week 12: Togetherness *Makes Time*   47
Week 13: Acceptance *Finds Good*   51
Week 14: Commitment *Teams Up*   55
Week 15: Communication *Questions*   59
Week 16: Conflict Resolution *Focuses*   63
Week 17: Forgiveness *Resolves*   67
Week 18: Emotional Intimacy *Speaks Candidly*   71
Week 19: Physical Intimacy *Romances*   75
Week 20: Spiritual Life *Reaches*   79

LEVEL THREE

Week 21: Love *Acts*   85
Week 22: Togetherness *Plays*   89
Week 23: Acceptance *Lets Go*   93
Week 24: Commitment *Gives*   97
Week 25: Communication *Chooses*   101
Week 26: Conflict Resolution *Replaces*   105
Week 27: Forgiveness *Restores*   109
Week 28: Emotional Intimacy *Hugs*   113
Week 29: Physical Intimacy *Excites*   117
Week 30: Spiritual Life *Locates*   123

LEVEL FOUR

Week 31: Love *Encourages*   129
Week 32: Togetherness *Converses*   133
Week 33: Acceptance *Stops Criticizing*   137
Week 34: Commitment *Disciplines*   141
Week 35: Communication *Cares*   145
Week 36: Conflict Resolution *Requires*   149
Week 37: Forgiveness *Absolves*   153
Week 38: Emotional Intimacy *Empathizes*   157
Week 39: Physical Intimacy *Communicates*   161
Week 40: Spiritual Life *Grows*   165

LEVEL FIVE

Week 41: Love *Serves*   171
Week 42: Togetherness *Bonds*   175
Week 43: Acceptance *Honors*   179
Week 44: Commitment *Clings To*   185
Week 45: Communication *Understands*   189
Week 46: Conflict Resolution *Surrenders*   193
Week 47: Forgiveness *Graces*   197
Week 48: Emotional Intimacy *Trusts*   201
Week 49: Physical Intimacy *Ministers*   205
Week 50: Spiritual Life *Enthrones*   209

Notes   213
The Top Ten Areas of Couple Life: A Cumulative Chart   218
Ledger for Couples   219

INTRODUCTION

Today's married couples have more timesaving devices and less time for each other than any other generation in America. Yet without time together, great marriages deteriorate into battlegrounds of demanding spouses fighting for the other's attention; good marriages become the flat, dull plains of couples starved for mountaintop experiences; and poor marriages become homes of desperation for couples coexisting "for the kids."

Time together is what makes marriage work. But how do you plan time together in your overly packed schedule of two jobs, two different shifts, picking up the kids from Grandma or the child-development center, while taking a night class for job advancement or spending more time in the air traveling than you do sleeping with your spouse?

You do it in snippets, slivers, fifteen-minute time slots carved out of the hard rock of your schedule, which will resist each chip of time you chisel out for your spouse. Fifteen minutes weekly—or the total of twelve and a half hours in one year.

"Sounds manageable, but will it make a difference in our marriage?" you ask.

It will make a difference because each chapter in this book delivers only one encapsulated truth and a practical to-do idea for impacting your thinking and changing the way you interact with your spouse during the week that follows each fifteen-minute segment.

Will you invest fifteen minutes a week to rediscover the cozy affection and intimate chats of your courtship days?

Will you find fifteen minutes a week for your peaceful but somewhat dull marriage to scale the heights of exhilaration?

Will you schedule fifteen minutes a week to rescue your marriage from the encroaching, venomous tentacles of divorce?

GETTING STARTED

So what steps do you take to your marriage-enhancing adventure? Here are ten suggestions to make it easier:

1. *Together decide whether you will read the lessons silently or switch off reading lessons aloud. We recommend the wife reads the odd-numbered lessons and the husband the even-numbered. The wife could also answer all questions first in the odd-numbered lessons and the husband in the even-numbered lessons.*
2. *During your fifteen minutes together, maintain body contact. Hold hands or sit side by side on a sofa, floor, or bed.*
3. *Relax. Take a deep breath, exhale today's cares and crises, and place them on the back burner of your mind.*
4. *Eliminate all distractions such as television, radio, and the phone. If you have children, schedule time after they are in bed.*
5. *Focus your full attention on your spouse.*
6. *Anticipate the pleasure of warm intimacy.*
7. *Allow approximately five minutes for reading and rereading, enough time to absorb the lesson ideas before discussing them with your spouse.*
8. *Risk being vulnerable. It's a small price to pay for a rejuvenated marriage.*
9. *Persevere. Schedule fifteen minutes with your spouse weekly. Keep to a regular, set time if possible. A broken promise communicates an uncaring heart. If you miss a week, ask for your spouse's forgivness and do two lessons the following week.*
10. *Resist the urge to skip around in this book to find something your spouse "needs to hear." Like warm-up exercises, this book's fifty lessons begin on a basic level and graduate to greater challenges, building on the previous level.*

Whether you've been married for one month or for fifty-one years, take each marriage energizer as directed. We are so certain you will have a more romantic, rewarding marriage that we guarantee it—or your money back (see page 223 for further information.)

You can achieve a lifetime of togetherness with a fifteen-minute weekly commitment to marriage enrichment. And as you work together toward a stronger, deeper couple life, remember this: Success in marriage consists not only in having the right spouse, but, more important, in becoming the right kind of spouse.

We'll keep you in our prayers.

Bobbie and Myron Yagel

HOW TO GET THE MOST OUT OF THIS BOOK

Whether you've been married one year or fifty-one years, *15 Minutes to Build a Stronger Marriage* is here to help you. After careful research in cataloging the indexes of over twenty-five twentieth-century marriage books, we have capsulized help in the ten areas that most impact a husband and wife:

love
togetherness
acceptance
commitment
communication
conflict resolution
forgiveness
emotional intimacy
physical intimacy
spiritual life

This book has five "levels" and moves from Level 1 (the most basic) to Level 5 (most advanced). Level 1 will address each of the ten areas in marriage. Then Level 2 will again address the ten areas, helping you build on what you learned in Level 1, and so on through Level 5. Because each lesson takes you deeper, it is important to start from the beginning of the book and work your way toward the back.

This book promises to help you and your spouse build a stronger, more intimate marriage with *only a fifteen-minute weekly commitment to marriage enrichment.* Each week features

- *practical and helpful information about the topic, along with interesting anecdotes from authors and well-known marriage experts like Ed Wheat, Walter Wangerin, Jr., Larry Crabb, and Dr. James Dobson.*

- *"For Stronger, Deeper Couple Life," which includes thought-provoking questions, fill-in statements, and exercises that are done with your spouse to enhance your marriage. Questions should be answered by both spouses, in turn, unless otherwise specified.*

- *"Putting (the topic) into Practice," which gives you a Scripture verse on which to reflect as well as a Challenge for the Week that will increase your understanding of each other and help you take small steps toward increased marital joy and relational harmony.*

As you complete each week's marriage energizer, flip to the "Ledger for Couples" (in the back of the book on pages 219–221), and fill in the date you completed the lesson, along with both of your initials. This ledger will help you keep track of your progress in the book as well as the dates on which you and your spouse made some exciting discoveries about each other and your marriage.

The "Top Ten Areas of Couple Life: A Cumulative Chart" (also listed at the back of the book on page 218) will give you an overview of where you're going and a review for whenever you need a refresher in a certain area of marriage.

You're just about ready to begin an exciting marriage adventure! However, before you jump in with both feet, we want you to think carefully about the following three conditions for success:

First, *both spouses must make a commitment of time.* Everyone's schedule is full. But spouses need to remember that others inwardly measure the genuineness of our love by the time carved out of busy schedules to spend together. Fifteen minutes a week—a mere twelve and a half hours a year—can make a tremendous difference in your marriage *if* both of you are committed. If you make this commitment together, it may mean getting out of bed at midnight on Saturday, saying, "We can't go to sleep. We haven't spent our fifteen minutes together this week." But that time will be well worth it.

Second, *both spouses must be interested in enhancing their marriage life.* It is important that one spouse not be perceived as the nag and the other as the uninterested procrastinator. If this happens, we recommend the procrastinator assume the responsibility of making sure a time is set and kept every week to do the exercises.

Third, *both spouses must take this commitment seriously.* A broken promise communicates an uncaring heart. If you miss a week (this should be extremely rare), ask for each other's forgiveness and then do two lessons the following week.

LEVEL ONE

LOVE
Speaks

I love you!"

With Myron's heartwarming words ringing in my ears, I returned his hug and kiss, but not his words.

Married only a few weeks, my new husband beamed down at me in my nightgown, with my frazzled, uncombed hair sticking straight up on my head. "Bobbie, I love you, and I know you love me too."

I understood why Myron spoke for me, but I didn't know whether he was trying to convince himself or me.

The words "I love you" seemed to stick in my throat. As hard as I tried, I seldom succeeded in speaking aloud the words I welcomed daily from Myron's lips.

Every time Myron said "I love you" to me, I checked my feelings to see if they registered warm and tingly enough to speak the words back to him. Lacking what I felt were the appropriate feelings, I remained silent.

Then, after attending our first marriage seminar, I learned that the engine that keeps marriage running is commitment. Feelings follow behind, like a caboose. Love is a decision I must make to seek the other's good. It asks not "How much must I do?" but "How much may I do for you today to meet your needs?"

When I discovered what love really was, I decided I would tell Myron I loved him, regardless of my feelings. Although I felt silly and hypocritical, I forced the words from my throat to my lips. Myron responded by showing me even greater love. I was amazed when my commitment to speak love to Myron daily actually brought warm feelings to my heart. I had acted my way to new feelings!

When was the last time you said "I love you!" to your spouse?

Research reveals that "one common symptom among couples who had broken up was that they never told each other 'I love you.'"[1]

Saying these three simple words three times a day will bond your marriage with superglue. The words are powerful, productive, and practical. When spoken warmly, they can arouse erotic physical desires, kindle romantic songs in our mind, or stimulate a heart celebration that shouts *Wow, I'm loved!*

If you can't remember the last time you said "I love you" to your spouse, make today the birthday of expressed love in your marriage. And you may want to add, as Myron does, "I love you, Bobbie, and I know you love me too!"

Acts of kindness never replace the assurance of being told we're loved. Many of our mothers and fathers sacrificed time, energy, and money to birth, train, educate, and prepare us for life. But most adult children who have been deprived of the verbal assurance of a parent's love would sacrifice almost any physical blessing to hear their parents say "I love you."

It is the same in marriage. We need to assure our spouse of our love by saying the awesome threesome: "I love you."

FOR STRONGER, DEEPER COUPLE LIFE

1. Ask each other the following questions:
   • How do you feel when I say "I love you"?

• Would you like for me to say "I love you" more often than I do?

2. Then share with each other the answer to this fill-in-the-blank statement: "I especially like your saying 'I love you' to me when . . ." (Examples: when you leave home, when you call me on the phone, when you come home, when we snuggle in bed, when you whisper in my ear at a party, etc.)

PUTTING LOVE INTO PRACTICE

Pleasant words are a honeycomb, sweet to the soul and healing to the bones.
PROVERBS 16:24

Challenge for the Week: Tell each other "I love you" three times daily. If possible, share those words at the special times your spouse identified as being most meaningful.

Caution: After this lesson, whenever your spouse says "I love you," ignore the urge to say "Oh, you're just saying that because our last lesson told you to" or "You don't mean that." Refusing spoken love will discourage your spouse from trying again.

Special note from the authors: Remember that the money-back guarantee is valid only if you and your spouse complete every week's study and fill out the Ledger for Couples (located at the back of the book).

TOGETHERNESS
Gazes

 One summer Sunday afternoon, as we cooled off in the pool adjoining our apartment complex, a couple nuzzling each other captured our attention.

"They're really in love," I whispered.

"What makes you think so?" Myron queried.

"Their gaze tells it all."

As we watched, the male removed his white baseball cap and perched it on his partner's head. After a long, adoring look, he swam backstroke across the pool, focusing his eyes on her between strokes. Many of his strokes turned into waves to his companion. This woman didn't have to ask her spouse if he adored her. His rapt attention communicated enough affection and appreciation to warm any woman's heart.

Have you ever sat in a booth across from a couple who couldn't quite focus on you while you spoke? Their eyes seemed drawn to each other with an unseen magnet of focused attention. Gazing on each other was an insatiable need.

Our eyes speak a love language of their own. As Ed Wheat says in his book *Love Life for Every Married Couple,* "Psychologists have found by controlled experiments that people who are deeply in love with each other engage in more eye contact than other couples. Eye contact shows its significance early in life when an infant's eyes begin focusing at about two to four weeks of age. From then on, a baby is always searching for another set of eyes to lock on to. . . . The child's emotions are fed by eye contact. We never outgrow this need."[2]

A few moments after I typed the above sentence, Myron returned from an errand. He entered my office to find me engrossed in writing. I looked up from my computer (although I wanted to keep typing) and kissed Myron (when I preferred ignoring him).

As he sat down, he chuckled and started telling me about a funny interview he had heard on the car radio; the guest had been talking about workaholics (like me). I turned around in my chair, forced myself to focus on Myron, and found myself laughing even as I longingly touched my computer. Repeatedly I fought the urge to look away from Myron to the screen of my unfinished chapter. Maintaining eye contact proved to be a greater challenge than I expected.

A few hours later I asked Myron if he had noticed anything different about me during that time. "I appreciated your undivided attention when I knew I had interrupted your writing. I felt warm and loved," he responded.

I was amazed. Although every muscle, thought, and desire in my body had to be denied to keep me from glancing back at my computer, I realized I had made Myron feel important with my eyes.

Even forced, deliberate eye contact has the power to satisfy two of the most basic human needs: love and acceptance.

FOR STRONGER, DEEPER COUPLE LIFE

As Cecil B. Murphey says, "God, the original lover, looks at us constantly. That's how lovers' eyes work—they constantly shift to the object of their love, shutting out everything else."[3]

1. Recall for your spouse a time when his or her rapt attention and tender looks evoked warm feelings of acceptance and love in you. Describe it in as much detail as you can remember. (Examples: when you spoke your marriage vows, when you catch your spouse's attention across a crowded room, when you admire each other's bodies during a time of intimacy, when you listen to each other's pain, etc.)
2. Then complete this sentence:
   "Your focused attention means the most to me when . . ."

PUTTING TOGETHERNESS INTO PRACTICE

The eyes of the Lord are on the righteous
and his ears are attentive to their cry.
PSALM 34:15

Challenge for the Week: When you listen to your spouse, maintain maximum eye contact. Become absorbed with what he or she is saying. Practice holding your gaze until your spouse is finished speaking.

ACCEPTANCE
Appreciates

H. Norman Wright prescribes for lovers a "One-a-Day Appreciation tablet . . . the most therapeutic capsule for healthy marriages. Each day tell your spouse one thing you especially appreciate about him or her. Doctor's advice: most effective when the mood is good and spouse isn't in a hurry."[4]

The appreciation factor in marriage faces its biggest challenge the first five minutes of every day. This time slot is crucial because it establishes the mood for the rest of the day. How much better to get in touch with a kiss, a few minutes of snuggling, or an endearing greeting like "Good morning, sweetheart," than to bump on the way to the bathroom and forget to speak, or in passing to ask a question such as "Did you remember to call and cancel Brittany's dentist appointment?" Although to-do lists are important for living, acknowledging our spouse should rank higher.

Affirmation is as simple as saying and doing whatever it takes to communicate to your spouse that he or she is number one in your life, someone you value and esteem above all others. Smiles of recognition, warm eye contact, hand pats, hugs, back rubs, a squeeze around the waist, or whispered endearments rank high as messengers of appreciation.

"Appreciation is an absolutely essential building block of life," write John and Linda Friel. "If you can honestly tell your partner that you feel blessed that he or she is in your life then you have something that is priceless . . . you have a kind of power that can endure all the arrows of outrageous fortune."[5]

Remember: The best way to appreciate your spouse is from dawn to dusk!

FOR STRONGER, DEEPER COUPLE LIFE

1. On a piece of paper, write ten things you appreciate about your spouse. (Examples: dimples, smile, hard work, leadership, cooking skills, sense of humor, faithfulness, parenting style, activities in church and community, etc.)
2. When both of you have finished writing, read your lists aloud to each other.
3. When you are sharing your list, make eye contact with your spouse before and after reading each point. When you are listening, remember to say "Thank you" to your spouse after each of the ten points.

PUTTING APPRECIATION INTO PRACTICE

Encourage one another daily.
HEBREWS 3:13

Challenge for the Week: Reread the list of affirmations you wrote about your spouse. As you begin to appreciate your spouse more for all he or she is and does, you will find it easier to affirm your spouse. Challenge yourself to say something affirming to your spouse daily!

COMMITMENT
Wills

Commitment is comparable to a roller-coaster ride. Once the ride starts, we're committed to the end. The decision has been made. The will is set. We thrill at the exhilarating highs. We tolerate the boring, flat sections of the ride. Nothing could convince us to disembark along the way!

Nearly every newlywed is advised by at least one gray-haired veteran of marriage that the highs won't last forever. Usually the couple smiles knowingly at one another, assured the intensity of their feelings is greater, deeper, and longer-lasting than that of any other newlyweds.

When the excitement wanes (from two days to two years, according to the experts), the couple may be devastated, thinking themselves no longer in love. This is simply not the case.

All changes stir the emotions, and the change from infatuation to attachment may include disappointment, anger, fear, and betrayal. When this happens it's important to know that our body chemistry is changing.

When two people "fall in love," researchers say that their bodies produce the chemical PEA (Phenylethylamine) that "whips the brain into a frenzy of excitement, which is why lovers feel euphoric, rejuvenated, optimistic and energized." When the stimulants subside, "a new group of chemicals take over . . . which calm and reassure. . . . . Its rewards of intimacy, dependability, warmth, empathy and shared experiences trigger the production of that mental comfort food, the endorphins."[6]

Staying aboard the roller coaster doesn't cancel our peak experiences. We have to expect highs and lows and realize that our love is not defined by those experiences. As James Dobson says, "A man and woman who love each other deeply and genuinely will naturally find themselves supercharged on one occasion and emotionally bland on another, but their love is not defined by the highs and lows. It is dependent on a commitment of the will."[7]

If the *will* sounds unromantic, consider this precious promise: "The longer two people have been married, the more likely it is that they'll stay married. Stability, friendship, familiarity, and affection are rewards the body clings to. As much as we love being dizzied by infatuation, such a state is stressful. It also feels magnificent to rest, to be free of anxiety or fretting and to enjoy one's life with a devoted companion."[8]

FOR STRONGER, DEEPER COUPLE LIFE

Charles Swindoll and his wife, Cynthia, strengthen their relationship by "declaring our permanent commitment to each other. Through the year, especially on New Year's Day, our anniversary, each other's birthday, we affirm our commitment eyeball to eyeball, stating our love and devotion to each other."[9]

1. Would this be a good practice for you to adopt as a couple? Why or why not? Discuss your response with your spouse.

2. Can you remember your wedding vows? If so, write them down and say them again to each other.

PUTTING COMMITMENT INTO PRACTICE

Therefore what God has joined together,
let man not separate.
MARK 10:9

Challenge for the Week: Make a date to watch your wedding video or look through your wedding album or photos.

COMMUNICATION
Listens

Norman Vincent Peale was nearly ninety-five when a friend described him as "the best listener": "Every time I have talked with Dr. Peale, he made me feel as if I was the only person in the room. How does he do it? His eyes are penetrating. His body language is still. His concentration is undistracted. I can tell that he's thinking about what I'm saying, rather than planning what he's going to say next. . . . Good listening requires true attentiveness."[10]

A priceless gift to give our spouse, one that keeps on giving, is for us to learn to listen "The Peale Way." In listening, we

- *interrelate,* experiencing something of what the other is experiencing emotionally
- *demonstrate our concern, caring, and compassion*
- *become consumed with each other.* In other words, we act as if we are dating. We hang on to every spoken word of our loved one. Our eyes study the other, oblivious of all surrounding activities.
- *free one another* to reveal hidden, sometimes even shameful

thoughts, events, or feelings. If we know the other will not criticize, judge, or put us down, we slowly open up. And then healing happens because we are fully understood by another!

• *help each other grow and change.* As Fay and Andre Bustanoby say, "When the listener touches the speaker where he hurts, an intimate bond of sharing is established. The listener has not judged the speaker, but rather has helped the speaker bear a burden. . . . [The listener] is no longer an adversary, but a friend and companion."[11]

There are seven skills involved in listening "The Peale Way":

1. *We involve our bodies.* A study by Philadelphia's Temple University indicated that only 7 percent of the message people receive from us is words; 38 percent is tone and 55 percent is nonverbal. [12]
2. *We stop every other activity* and make some sort of physical gesture to show we are listening (perhaps we put our arm around our spouse or hold his or her hand). We refuse to allow our eyes the freedom to wander. The television, radio, and CD player remain off.
3. *We maintain an upbeat tone* that communicates "Keep talking."
4. *We keep a relaxed, frown-free face* that communicates an openness to listen.
5. *We tune in to nonverbal cues,* noting our spouse's body posture, emotional state, and voice inflection. We ask ourselves, Does my spouse look relaxed? uptight? angry? What messages are my spouse's eyes giving? Are they nervously darting, glaring, crestfallen, warm, friendly, brimming with tears? Does his or her voice sound anxious, depressed, optimistic? Is he or she frowning, smiling, or worrying? Listening demands focused attention.

6. *We respond to feelings* without criticism or judgment.
7. *We are slow to speak.*

The essential question of listening is not how good a listener we think we are but how good a listener our spouse finds us to be. We must know the answer to this question if we want to grow in understanding and intimacy.

FOR STRONGER, DEEPER COUPLE LIFE

As you ask each other the following questions, be especially aware of your spouse's body language and what you convey through your own body language.

1. Do I listen to you:
   • most of the time?
   • occasionally?
   • seldom?

Explain why you feel this way, or recall an example to share with your spouse. (This exercise works best if the person asking the question refrains from commenting on the answer.)

2. Read the seven skills needed to listen "The Peale Way." After each skill, ask each other, "How do I do with this one? What could I change to become a better listener?"

Caution: This is not a time to criticize but a time to suggest improvements. Remain positive and affirming.

PUTTING LISTENING INTO PRACTICE

Dear brothers [and sisters], don't ever forget that it is best to listen much, speak little, and not become angry.
JAMES 1:19, TLB

Challenge for the Week: Write down the ways your spouse suggested that you could improve your listening skills. Then try to practice at least one of those skills now and in the weeks to come.

CONFLICT RESOLUTION
Chooses

M.any professionals believe we have only two possible responses to conflict in marriage:

- We may choose to withdraw and protect ourselves from pain.
- We may choose to reach out and gain understanding of our spouse and ourselves.

Drs. John and Margaret Paul contend that "every interaction with people in our lives is governed by these two intentions. . . . We can choose protection one moment and learning the next, but the two are mutually exclusive. We cannot be protected (closed, hard, defensive) and open to learning (open, soft, curious) at the same time."[13]

Conflict arises when spouses differ in what they desire, feel, or think. You may desire to talk when I want to mow the lawn; you may want sex when I need sleep; you may feel like stretching out in front of the television when I want a family swim.

Since we have different desires, feelings, and thoughts, conflict is inevitable in marriage. But conflict must not be viewed as bad or as a sign of failure. Rather, it is an opportunity to gain greater understanding of ourselves as well as our spouse.

Conflict has a way of finding us out. It may reveal that we are immature, too threatened to listen, and fearful of hearing anything different from what we believe and think we need. In this self-protective mode, we belittle, criticize, or judge with unkind, untrue accusations, such as:

- "You always have to be right."
- "You never care about what I feel."
- "How can you think that?"
- "There you go again. Same old rubbish!"
- "That's the dumbest thing I ever heard."

Conflict may also prove us to be mature, caring, and good listeners. Whenever we remain in the presence of the one we feel like avoiding, conflict becomes a stepping-stone to maturity. We learn to speak softly in a nonaccusatory tone and to ask questions or make statements that will increase our understanding, such as:

- "Please tell me more."
- "I want to understand how you feel."
- "I didn't know you felt like that."
- "I'm so sorry I hurt you when I said that."
- "This must be hard for you."

Every conflict provides us with a priceless opportunity to grow closer together in intimacy . . . and to understand more what makes us, our spouse, and our relationship tick.

FOR STRONGER, DEEPER COUPLE LIFE

1. When you hear the word *conflict*, which of the following words come to mind?
   - opportunity
   - failure
   - growth
   - rejection
   - good
   - misunderstanding
   - anger
   - coldness
   - intimacy
   - losing or winning

   Which of these words describe how you want to respond to your next marital conflict? Or you can come up with a word of your own.

2. Do you agree that there are only two ways to respond to conflict: to draw within to protect ourselves from pain, or to reach out to learn about our spouse as well as ourselves? Why or why not? If not, can you think of another option?
3. As a couple, where would you like to be in your conflict resolution eight months from now?

PUTTING CONFLICT RESOLUTION INTO PRACTICE

Be patient with each other, making allowance for each other's faults because of your love.
EPHESIANS 4:2, TLB

Challenge for the Week: Take time to reread this lesson privately. Ask your heavenly Father to show you the ways in which you most often respond to conflict. Then ask him to help you make whatever changes are necessary to improve the conflict resolution in your marriage.

FORGIVENESS
Touches

After a couple had been married for a number of years, they recalled this experience from their dating days: "'We had a terrible row,' he said. 'We yelled at each other and I stormed off.' He paused and looked at his wife. 'Honey, do you remember what we argued about?'

"She thought for a minute and said, 'No, I don't. I only remember that when you walked away, I ran after you, and that ended it.'"[14]

Imagine what would have happened if this wise woman had not pursued her lover. Their relationship would have been threatened by two people's digging in their heels, crossing their arms, stiffening their bodies, setting their mouths in a pout, and going home to engrave the memory on a mental wall of self-righteousness.

The few feet dividing us may quickly become the Grand Canyon of hostility if we refuse each other's touch. Forgiveness requires a decision to span the cavern of separation with an outreached arm to clutch a hand, stroke a head, hug a shoulder, or caress a face.

One of the best ways for spouses to preclude angry eruptions in marriage is for one of us to touch the other the moment we sense trouble brewing. This way, we interrupt the separation before it occurs. It's almost impossible to hate someone whose hand you hold.

Unforgiveness is a total body illness whose pain is emotional as well as physical. Sometimes we grasp onto unforgiveness as if it holds a rich reward for us. But the only rewards of this enemy of wholeness are headaches, stress, heartburn, ulcers, arthritis flare-ups, and more.

The longer we reject each other when we're hurt and angry, the more difficult it becomes to bridge the chasm of separation and forgive. This is why the apostle Paul warns us, "Do not let the sun go down while you are still angry" (Ephesians 4:26).

To touch is to communicate our acceptance of the other even as he or she speaks harshly, accuses falsely, behaves unkindly, or acts inconsiderately. One of our primary needs is to know we're loved and accepted by our spouse when we least deserve it. And that's something good lovers communicate by touching.

FOR STRONGER, DEEPER COUPLE LIFE

For this exercise, one of you needs to be the "answering" spouse, the other the "listening" spouse. Then switch roles and do the exercise again.

1. The "answering" spouse answers the following question:
   When I'm irritated, angry, and withdrawing from you, I wish you would
   a. run after me
   b. hug me
   c. leave me alone for five minutes. Then I'll come back and touch you.
   d. ask my forgiveness for what you did that I allowed to make me angry
   e. kiss me and refuse to let me run away
   f. reach out and hold my hand
   g. other (fill in the blank) _____

The listening spouse clarifies by asking, "Are you saying that when you're mad at me, you want me to . . . ?"

2. Identify the ways in which you may have chosen to hold on to anger and refused an offered touch by:
   • pouting
   • withdrawing
   • withholding sex
   • turning a cold shoulder
   • answering with abrupt, one-word answers to questions
   • giving the silent treatment
   • cooling affection
   • not listening
   • lashing out
   • other (fill in the blank)_____

3. Consider making this promise to your spouse: "I'll make every effort to stop using these defensive tactics when you respond with a tender touch. I'll stay with you and talk out our disagreement."

PUTTING FORGIVING TOUCHES INTO PRACTICE

Get rid of all bitterness, rage and anger, brawling and
slander, along with every form of malice. Be kind and
compassionate to one another, forgiving each other,
just as in Christ God forgave you.
EPHESIANS 4:31-32

Challenge for the Week: When your spouse is angry and you feel like distancing yourself, reach out and touch him or her. The healing power of forgiveness is at your fingertips.

EMOTIONAL INTIMACY
Opens Up

Pastor and author William Coleman writes, "Every heart should have ears. The ears on our head collect information, but the ears on our heart tune in for feelings." [15]

People who listen with their head say things like:

- "Life has problems, you know."
- "So what's the big deal? Just call off the party and get on with life."
- "Well, what are you going to do about it?"
- "I know exactly what you're saying."

People who listen with their heart say things like:

- "Oh no. How terrible."
- "You sound as if you're really angry."
- "Do I hear you saying you've had it? You want out?"
- "Am I right that you're feeling lonely, left behind?"

Intimacy originates with our willingness to be transparent. When we reveal a secret desire, disclose a hidden thought, or divulge a private emotion, we open up to one another on an intimate level.

Intimacy comes from the Latin *intimus,* meaning "inmost." Spouses may know all about the foods the other relishes, how the other rates as a sex partner, where the other is going tomorrow, what the other enjoys most about work, but still not know much about his or her inmost being, what he or she is really thinking.

Working toward emotional intimacy means we need to learn to listen to each other with our hearts as well as our heads. We may choose to ignore the underlying passions of our lives and communicate strictly on an intellectual level. But is this all we want or expect from marriage? We hope not!

For emotional intimacy to take root and grow in our garden of love, we need two spouses who are willing

- to be vulnerable and share secret thoughts or reveal hidden emotions
- to listen with kindness and compassion to shared thoughts and emotions
- to receive respectfully all revealed thoughts and emotions without judgment, criticism, or belittling. (We must choose not to say, "How in the world could you think *that?"*)

In most marriages, one spouse shares thoughts and emotions with greater ease than the other. Jay Kesler explains why husbands sometimes agonize more about vulnerability than wives: "Men have been trained to be guarded in expressing their innermost thoughts and feelings. Many men feel that life is like a terribly competitive poker game in which they must never betray what they're really feeling, lest another person know what's in their hand and somehow do them in. . . . They are often closed and unable to share their emotions and personal thoughts, not even with their wives."[16]

Intimacy doesn't spring up like a weed in a garden, with little or no effort. It's more like a fragile flower, intentionally planted in a greenhouse of love where it will be nurtured and sheltered.

FOR STRONGER, DEEPER COUPLE LIFE

As you ask one another the following questions, listen carefully for the responses—they may not be what you think. Accept all of your spouse's answers as true for him or her.

1. How do you feel about discussing intimacy with me? Do you feel threatened, hopeless, anxious, expectant, scared, joyful, ignorant, successful, unsuccessful, or _____ (fill in the blank)? Why?

2. Which of the following three conditions for spousal intimacy would give you the most trouble? Why?
    • to be vulnerable and share secret thoughts or reveal hidden emotions
    • to listen with kindness and compassion to shared thoughts and emotions
    • to receive respectfully all revealed thoughts and emotions without judgment, criticism, or belittling

3. Choose either *(a)* or *(b)* below. Then talk about the subjects listed on a more emotional than factual level for one minute.
    a. How did you feel growing up with your parents/brothers/sisters/any other live-in relative?
    b. What emotions do you have when you hear the following words?
        • circus
        • my favorite pet
        • Christmas
        • fishing
        • allowance

- ice-cream cone
- Barbie dolls
- teasing
- fighting

PUTTING EMOTIONAL INTIMACY INTO PRACTICE

Therefore, as God's chosen people, holy and dearly loved,
clothe yourselves with compassion, kindness, humility,
gentleness and patience.
COLOSSIANS 3:12

Challenge for the Week: The next time your spouse reports something to you, listen carefully. Are there unspoken emotions behind the factual sharing? If so, try to draw out the other's emotions with reflective sentences, such as "You sound wonderfully happy (or terribly angry) about what happened."

If we misname the other's emotion, the one speaking may correct us with something like "No, honey, I don't feel mad. But I do feel ignored, overlooked, and unhappy."

PHYSICAL INTIMACY
Strokes

The bottom line of physical touch is that our marriage won't survive without it. Physical intimacy strokes, snuggles, squeezes, kisses, caresses, and hugs daily, satisfying the other's skin hunger.

Formulas abound for touching and hugging. Virgil Satir recommends "four hugs a day for survival, eight for maintenance and twelve for growth."[17]

A UCLA research project determined that meaningful touch is essential to forming and maintaining an intimate relationship. It said a woman, in particular, needs eight to ten meaningful touches daily for physical and mental health.

Our touches need not be limited to hugs or to any one area of our spouse's body. The human body has "tiny, tactile receptors" located throughout it. "When those receptors are touched or pressed, nerves carry impulses to the brain. The brain interprets these impulses, and we perceive that the thing that touched us is warm or cold, hard or soft. It causes pain or pleasure. We may also interpret it as loving or hostile."[18] It is wherever we find those tiny, tactile receptors arranged in clusters that our bodies are most sensitive to touch, such as our fingertips and the tip of our tongue.

Understanding the physiological aspect of touching does not necessarily make us a good lover. We must learn and practice touches most pleasing to our spouse, the warm, cuddly kind and the sensuously sexual ones.

Ann Landers polled her female readers to learn if they would be content to be held close and treated tenderly and forget about the sexual act. Of the more than ninety thousand women responding, 72 percent answered yes; 40 percent of this group was younger than forty.

The multifaceted messages of human touch are summed up by Cecil Murphey when he talks about his wife, Shirley: "When I touch Shirley and she allows it, there is a commitment established. When I put my arm around Shirley, one of the things my actions say is, 'I'm here, actually present with you. My mind is not on tomorrow's problems or today's leftover business.'

"Lovers listen with their hands. A gentle stroking or a warm touch opens up the other and says, 'It's all right for you to be free with me. I'm here and I'm listening.'

"When I hold Shirley's hand and she's talking, I respond unconsciously by the pressure of my fingers. When she's not feeling her best, she may put her head on my shoulder, and I stroke her hair. My fingers say, 'It's all right, honey.'

"Lovers' hands communicate when there are no words to be said. They sometimes speak even stronger than words."[19]

FOR STRONGER, DEEPER COUPLE LIFE

Spend time with your spouse doing the following "touching" exercise (then swap roles and try it again):

1. Touch your spouse as you want to be touched, demonstrating how and where you prefer to be kissed, touched, rubbed, stroked, massaged, etc.

2. Have your spouse spend three minutes kissing, touching, rubbing, stroking, and massaging in ways you have demonstrated.

PUTTING PHYSICAL INTIMACY INTO PRACTICE

His left arm is under my head, and
his right arm embraces me.
SONG OF SONGS 2:6

Challenge for the Week: Hug your spouse daily and often, adding nonsexual touching. Nightly, before falling asleep, talk about how you felt that day as you were physically touched more often.

SPIRITUAL LIFE
Blesses

Pluck any man out of a church pew on Sunday morning and liken him to a neighbor who's still at home, poring through the two-pound Sunday newspaper in his easy chair. Let's say the two are the same age and earn comparable salaries. Neither of them smokes, drinks, or plays the lottery. Both floss their teeth, collect baseball cards, and enjoy cheesecake.

"Which man will live longer and enjoy the benefits of a stable marriage? Answer: The man [or woman] in the pew. In recent years, scientific research is backing up what common sense has told us for years; mainly, that churchgoers live longer, stay married and feel happier than those who say they don't believe in God. . . . Science is merely verifying what Scripture has told us for centuries: 'The fear of the Lord adds length to life' and 'He [or she] who finds a wife [or husband], finds a good thing.'"[20]

In this same article Larson and Mary Ann Mayo report, "People who attend church even once a month increase their chances of staying married. Religion provides couples with a shared sense of values, ideology and purpose in life. Christianity provides support for married couples to be committed, to show respect, to be emotionally supportive, to communicate effectively, and creates a stable power structure for the home. This intimacy solidifies a marriage romantically and sexually."[21]

Spiritual life blesses in many ways—one of them surprising. Author Kevin Leman has said, "Sex begins in church!" The studies of Larson and Mary Ann Mayo also uncovered facts that run counter to what most people think about sexual intimacy: "The most religious women were most satisfied with the 'frequency of intercourse and felt free to discuss sex openly with their husbands, and, most surprisingly, were more orgasmic than were the nonreligious.'"[22]

There is one more consideration for the blessings of spiritual life: "Remember this: with money you can build a house; add love to that house and you have a home; add God to that home and you have a temple."[23]

FOR STRONGER, DEEPER COUPLE LIFE

1. What was your family's attitude toward church?
2. What adjectives would you choose to describe your relationship with God?
   - great
   - distant
   - lonely
   - warm
   - satisfying
   - content
   - shallow
   - deep
   - other (fill in the blank)_____

3. How do you feel about your present level of church involvement?

4. It has been said that Christianity is not a religion but a relationship. On a scale of 1 to 10 (10 being very close and 1 being distant), how close are you to Jesus Christ? How close would you like to be?
5. In what area would you most like to grow spiritually?

End your time together by holding hands for a moment of silent prayer about the spiritual aspect of your marriage.

PUTTING OUR SPIRITUAL LIFE INTO PRACTICE

You will seek me and find me when
you seek me with all your heart.
JEREMIAH 29:13

Challenge for the Week: Seek God together at least once this week, praying specifically, "Lord Jesus, we would like to know you better."

LEVEL TWO

LOVE
Speaks and Discovers

One summer night Myron arrived home at 11:30 P.M. from a marathon church meeting. I gasped in delight as he held out a freshly cut, mammoth magnolia blossom. The bloom's delicate, perfumed fragrance permeated the kitchen as I rushed to place it in a vase of water.

I hugged Myron as enthusiastically as if I had just opened a crushed velvet box displaying a 14-carat gold necklace. All week, on rides around Richmond, I had sighed at each sighting of a towering magnolia dressed in snow-white blooms, always on someone else's property. Myron had remembered my longing and had snitched a bloom from a tree branch overhanging a fence.

I cherish this late-night memory because it met one of my primary love needs, surprise gifts! I need to know I remain in his thoughts when he's away from me.

On the other hand, Myron's greatest love needs are sexual fulfillment and spoken affirmations (no criticism, please!).

In *His Needs, Her Needs,* William Harley, Jr., lists a man's five most basic love needs as

1. sexual fulfillment
2. recreational companionship
3. an attractive spouse
4. domestic support
5. admiration

He lists a woman's most basic needs as

1. affection
2. conversation
3. honesty and openness
4. financial support
5. family commitment[1]

Gary Chapman lists our five primary love needs as

1. *words of affirmation:* "You look handsome in that suit." "I'm so proud of you!" "Wow! Salesperson of the year!"
2. *quality time:* uninterrupted intervals with focused attention and listening ears
3. *receiving gifts* that speak of love
4. *acts of service:* Instead of you doing chores, your spouse out of love or concern does the chores for you, such as writing checks, helping with after-party cleanup, running errands.
5. *physical touch:* holding hands, back rubs, cuddling close, sexual intercourse, etc.[2]

As we move on to reveal our primary love needs to one another, we need to remember that, in disclosing a need, we become vulnerable and open to the pain of having that need neglected or ignored by our spouse.

Many things asked of you in this lesson may cause temporary pain. That is the price we pay for intimacy. But an intimate marriage is worth hurting for.

Because of the ease of causing our spouse pain, when we finish this lesson, we'll need to record in indelible ink the other's acknowledged love needs and practice meeting them as often as possible.

FOR STRONGER, DEEPER COUPLE LIFE

1. Take turns completing the following sentence: "I guess that you feel most loved when I . . ." When you are the listener, refrain from commenting or using body language that shows disbelief or disagreement.
2. Then silently reflect on these personal questions:
   - How do I most often express my love to my spouse? (The things you do for your spouse possibly indicate what you would like your spouse to do for you.)
   - Reread Harley's and Chapman's lists of love needs. Recall what your spouse suggested as your greatest love need. Is he or she right? From your reading and thinking, what seems to be your greatest love need(s)?
3. When you are ready to share your greatest love need(s), squeeze your spouse's hand and complete the following sentence aloud for your spouse: "I think I feel most loved when you . . ."
4. The listening spouse then should respond by completing the following sentence: "If I want to make you feel really loved, it would be best for me to . . ."

PUTTING LOVE INTO PRACTICE

For if you give [to meet your spouse's love needs], you will get! Your gift will return to you in full and overflowing

*measure, pressed down, shaken together to make
room for more, and running over. Whatever measure
you use to give—large or small—will be used to
measure what is given back to you.*
LUKE 6:38, TLB

Challenge for the Week: Choose one of your spouse's revealed love
needs and meet it at least once in the next few days.

TOGETHERNESS
Gazes and Makes Time

Does your romance need rekindling? Is your marriage rooted in routine? Are you weary, worn out, and wishing for something magical to happen?

An overwhelming number of marriage counselors recommend resuming regular, planned dating as the solution for "marriage blahs." Weekly dating is highly recommended; biweekly is considered minimal. Marriage without dates is like courtship without caresses.

"It's important to rekindle your early courtship behaviors, the things you did together that you now miss," writes *Marriage Partnership*'s columnist Jay Kesler. "And not just the date nights and the fun things you used to do, but the spontaneity and the silly things you did with each other. When we get married we tend to start buying kitchen appliances and air conditioners and alternators for the car; but occasionally we need to remember the personal touches. . . . And we need to take time to be together and discover what's new about this person we married."[3]

If you and your spouse don't date regularly, check or circle any of the following reasons you give for not doing so:

- kids' activities require full-time chauffeuring
- overtime at work
- no money
- too exhausted
- we don't have fun together anymore
- separate activities separate us
- too many outside commitments
- haven't taken the time to plan dates
- put everything else before our togetherness
- not enough shared interests to date

Excuses are like trying to float with weights tied to our feet. If we don't get rid of them, our marriage may sink to the bottom.

No money? Enjoy a bubble bath together by candlelight.

No time? Sit outdoors for fifteen minutes, after the kids are in bed, sipping your favorite refreshment and studying the sky for interesting constellations.

Kids? Ask friends to baby-sit yours in their house and return home for twenty-four hours together, minus beepers, phone, radio, or television. (And make sure you return your friends' favor!)

No fun together anymore? Take a break from your normal schedule. Check into a local motel with only toothbrushes, perfume, and each other. Spend the night with the television off. Cuddle in each other's arms and remember your most romantic dates before marriage.

Throughout our marriage, we've enjoyed getaway weekends, minus family or friends. Just us. Together. We've experienced everything from two weeks in Bermuda to two nights in a friend's vacated home without radio, television, or furniture. We hauled in a mattress to sleep on, feasted on McDonald's food, strolled through the woods, and spent extended hours in bed. Even now that we're retired, with an empty nest, we've continued our getaways. We like being together alone, with nothing to divert us from our shared love.

Luxuriating in each other's undivided attention may be a rare commodity if calendars are full of appointments. A weekend away may be what we need for rekindling romance. But a one-hour date at an ice-cream parlor will also build a sense of togetherness as we caress one another with our eyes, hold hands, and recall an especially romantic memory. Try sitting together on the same side of the booth.

For Stronger, Deeper Couple Life

1. Do you agree with the marriage counselors who insist that dating is the best way to rekindle romance? Why or why not?
2. Take a look at your personal calendar of activities. Does it agree with your beliefs? If not, why not?
3. Discuss together what you both see as the obtacles to making dates with your spouse. Do you think they're valid enough to disregard the advice of the experts and forget about the romance dating adds to a relationship?

Caution: If you are the "listening" spouse, resist the temptation to disagree with your spouse's reasons for not making a date. Also resist answering for your spouse or introducing a reason he or she has not mentioned, such as golf, shopping, fishing, fitness center, etc.

4. Share your responses as you fill in the blanks to these two statements:

• Some of my favorite dates with you were . . .

• They were favorites because . . .

Putting Togetherness into Practice

My lover spoke and said to me, "Arise, my darling, my
beautiful one, and come with me."
SONG OF SONGS 2:10

Challenge for the Week: Take turns planning one date each for the next four weeks. Consider making one a mystery date that keeps your spouse in suspense.

ACCEPTANCE
Appreciates and Finds Good

Seldom do two people ever get to a wedding ceremony unless they have been appreciating the good traits of each other and looking for the best in each other. . . . The positive characteristics in the other person matched our needs and we not only recognized them but we praised the other person for them. Without even thinking, we became a 'good finder'—noticing and finding the good, the strengths in the other person and expecting the best results."[4]

Sadly, as time marches on in marriage, finding good is replaced by finding fault. We begin to criticize the very character traits we once praised as strengths. Usually these are also the character traits we lack, the character strengths we need from our spouse to complete our personality.

If we are easily frazzled, we might criticize the other's stability and lack of emotional display; if we're obsessive about neatness, we might disparage the other's lack of organization; if we're the "bright idea" person who initiates most activities, we might judge the other's lack of

51

creativity; if we're the uptight spouse, we might attack the other's laid-back style.

When judgment overthrows the throne of appreciation, the very foundation of marriage is threatened. We must never allow criticism to replace finding good.

In our earlier married years, I (Bobbie) quickly became Myron's expert faultfinder and my own devoted admirer! I considered him my lump of clay to pinch, squeeze, and remold into my fairy-tale image of the strong, assertive male (who would never have been able to last a week married to assertive, iron-willed me). I fully ignored his powerful strengths of gentleness, humility, and steadiness, all of which I lacked. Those very characteristics that attracted him to me were the things I criticized in marriage, seeing them as weaknesses in my spouse.

Today, with God's help, I'm Myron's "good finder." I need all of my husband's strengths to complete me, just as he needs my spontaneous, organized, and outgoing personality to complete him. Myron, in his humility, has accepted me as completing him since the day we married.

James Dobson tells a story about a surgeon who was standing by the bedside of a young woman, "Her face postoperative, her mouth twisted by palsy, clownish. A tiny twig of the facial nerve, the one to the muscles of her mouth, has been severed.

"'Will my mouth always be like this?' she asks.

"'Yes,' I say, 'it will.'

"She nods and is silent. But the young husband smiles.

"'I like it,' he says. 'It's kind of cute.'

"Unmindful, he bends to kiss her crooked mouth, and I can see how he twists his own lips to accommodate hers, to show her that their kiss still works. I hold my breath and let the wonder [of finding good] in."[5]

That woman had something all spouses long for: unconditional love and acceptance.

FOR STRONGER, DEEPER COUPLE LIFE

1. What are the first things that attracted you to your spouse?
2. Which of your spouse's strengths do you lack? How do those strengths help to "complete" you?
3. When did one of your spouse's strengths help you get through a tough time? Describe what happened.

PUTTING ACCEPTANCE INTO PRACTICE

Accept one another, then, just as Christ accepted you.
ROMANS 15:7

Challenge for the Week: Each day ask yourself, Am I my spouse's "good finder" or have I become a "faultfinder"?

COMMITMENT
Wills and Teams Up

Happy couples team up. Whenever one is up to bat, the other cheers. They have a team mentality, doing as many things together as possible, like eating, playing, working, vacationing, sleeping, joking, praying, and reading.

Clinical psychologist Willard F. Harley, Jr., believes that if a wife is to feel close to her husband, as when they dated, he needs to give her up to fifteen hours weekly of undivided attention. In writing to men, Harley says:

1. I have my sphere of interests, and my spouse has hers. If these do not overlap, we can only grow farther and farther apart.
2. Because there are only so many hours in the day and week, I have to choose: I can pursue interests that we share, or I can pursue interests we do not share. If I do the latter, we will grow apart. If I do the former, we will grow together.
3. As I gain interests that are my spouse's interests, we have much more to talk about. Conversation becomes easier and

more interesting. I can meet her need for conversation with less and less effort. It becomes natural and spontaneous.[6]

We may not be able to spend fifteen hours a week with our spouses, but if we're flexible, we may add minutes to every day's togetherness. Consider teaming up by

- *driving together* to different appointments and meetings. One spouse's meeting or appointment may start earlier and the other's end later. The total distance traveled may be greater, but the communication time gained will be worth it. We know, because it works for us. Although we've added a good forty minutes by driving together where we used to drive separately (church, dentist's office), the driving time furnishes an opportunity to talk, enjoy music together, or touch in meaningful ways.
- *going to bed together.* Our body clocks differ. Myron retires early to arise early. I prefer staying up until midnight and sleeping in. So almost every night we split the time difference and climb into bed together, each of us willing to give a little to gain snuggle time.
- *cleaning up together.* Team up to clean up after a party or meal, and let relaxed chatting turn a chore into fun.
- *taping favorite television shows to watch together later.* Bleep out commercials when viewing, and then turn off the television and talk together in the bonus minutes saved by not watching commercials.
- *compromising to make it work.* I prefer to walk alone so that I can pray. Myron prefers my companionship on daily walks. So we compromise, walking one mile together and the second alone.

At first, teaming up was very threatening for me. But slowly I'm learning to say no to my independent nature in order to join the search for together time. The result? Our marriage is more romantic, more healthy, and more fun!

FOR STRONGER, DEEPER COUPLE LIFE

1. Make a list of all the activities you presently drive to separately—or the tasks you do separately. Discuss which of these you might be able to do together.
2. Out of the activities named in brainstorming, choose two small tasks to try doing together in the upcoming month.
3. Finish this sentence for your spouse: "I'm most happy with you by my side when we . . ."

PUTTING TEAMWORK INTO PRACTICE

Love does not insist on its own way.
1 CORINTHIANS 13:5, RSV

Challenge for the Week: Make an unpleasant task fun by doing it together lightheartedly.

COMMUNICATION
Listens and Questions

W endell Johnson once noted, "We are our own most enchanted listeners. No one speaks as well on such interesting topics as we do. If we could listen just to ourselves, listening would be no problem."

Humanly, we prefer speaking over listening. While making a somewhat feeble attempt to hear what the other is saying, our thoughts, problems, jokes, and anecdotes race about in our heads, waiting to spill out. The result? As Paul Tournier says, "Listen to all the conversations of our world, between nations as well as those between couples. They are, for the most part, dialogues of the deaf."[7]

All too often we listen to interrupt, to correct, to make a point, to talk about our interests. All too seldom do we listen intently to really hear and understand. Asking our spouse three questions before we interrupt the conversational flow to talk about ourselves offers us one excellent way to improve our listening skills.

The "three-question technique" provides a quick listening checkup to keep us from focusing attention on ourselves while listening. With this technique we listen intently enough to be able to ask three questions before we say "I" or before we switch the conversation to our perspective, interests, or problems. In this technique, we sometimes substitute a reflective sentence, such as "Sounds as if you had fun," "That must have been awesome," or "Tell me more," to keep the attention focused on the speaker.

Following are three attempts at the "three-question technique":

Attempt #1

Husband: "I had a great day today!"

Wife: "That's nice. I had a lousy one."

Oops! The wife just flunked the "three-question technique" because she said "I" without even asking her husband one question. She piggybacked the subject introduced by her husband, using it as a springboard to talk about her day.

Attempt #2

Husband: "I had a great day today!"

Wife: "I'm so glad. What did you do?"

Husband: "David called and asked me out to the farm. Wanted me to see their English setter's litter of pups."

Wife: "That's nice. All I had was a litter of problems."

Oops! One question beats none. Let's try again.

Attempt #3

Husband: "I had a great day today!"

Wife: "I'm so glad. What did you do?" *(Question one)*

Husband: "David called and asked me out to the farm. Wanted me to see their English setter's litter of pups."

Wife: "Hey, I'll bet they're cute." *(Question two is a door-opener statement, a response that says, "Keep talking. I'm interested.")*

Husband: "All six are perfect. Even more important, David and I had time to clear up our long-standing problem."

Wife: "That was important to you, wasn't it?" *(Question three)*

Husband: "Yes. David's friendship means a lot. I've felt unsettled since we quarreled last month. I think our friendship's back on track. I feel great!"

Think of how much the wife would have missed learning about her spouse if she had jumped in with her agenda without asking even one question. Asking three questions helps us get to the heart of the speaker, where the underlying emotions or problems lie.

The subject we first introduce in conversation is called "the presenting problem," and it's seldom the real problem.

The sample conversation above began with the husband sharing a fact: "David called." But it ended with the resolution of the real problem: He and his friend had quarreled and now were back on track.

The wife in Attempt #3 gave her husband love's seldom-offered gift: listening! And in listening she mined the riches of his heart and hit pure gold.

FOR STRONGER, DEEPER COUPLE LIFE

In this exercise, one spouse is the "speaker"; the other is the "listener." Then reverse roles and try it again.

Speaker: "Honey, let me tell you about the most pleasant day I ever spent with you." Try to share for two to three minutes.

Listener: Ask a minimum of three questions and/or reflective sentences to gather as much information as possible about why this day brought your spouse pleasure.

Caution: Dates, days, times, and sequence of events are not important in this exercise, so correcting your spouse is unnecessary.

Putting Communication into Practice

But blessed are your eyes because they see,
and your ears because they hear.
MATTHEW 13:16

Challenge for the Week: Count to three each time you question your spouse about the topic of conversation he or she initiated.

CONFLICT RESOLUTION
Chooses and Focuses

I remember our first lovers' quarrel. Perched side by side on our high Colonial bed, feet dangling over the side, I looked into Myron's troubled eyes and asked, "What's wrong?"

I can still picture Myron in his rumpled blue pajamas with one side of the collar standing up. His head hung low. "Well, I'm sure it's nothing, but I need to hear from you that it's not true."

"Hear what?" I demanded, dropping Myron's hand.

"Well, my mother told me this wild story about you and Jimmy Yates and some lovers' rendezvous in the country. Just tell me it didn't happen, and I'll be okay."

"You mean I have to reassure you I haven't been unfaithful to you whenever your paranoid mother comes up with another one of her crazy stories?"

Jumping to the floor, I grabbed my pillow, marched out of the bedroom, and slammed the door behind me. I spent the night on the sofa, weeping alone. Because I was hurt so deeply, I distanced myself from Myron to protect myself from more pain. I also hoped he felt punished.

The truth is, I punished only myself. At least once a week I dug deeply into the dumpster of hurtful memories to remind Myron of his failure. I never wanted him to forget how he unfairly questioned my faithfulness to him. Distraught with pain and ignorant of how to stop the ugly memories whirling in my mind night and day, I suffered an acute depression. My refusal to let go of the past cost me physically and emotionally and robbed our marriage of maximum joy for eight years.

I ended my eight-year ordeal by welcoming the Lord Jesus Christ into my heart to forgive all my sins. It took months for me to face my interminably long list of failures for which I needed Jesus to forgive me. He did, and I was set free to focus on Myron and forgive him of his one failure. How warm and wonderful it felt to return to life lived in the sunshine of today.

Because I know personally the high cost of punishing another by refusing to let go of past hurtful events, I have learned to forgive soon after we hurt each other, and I seldom, if ever, go to bed angry. Our living room sofa has never again served as a bed for an angry spouse.

Have you ever spoiled today with yesterday's pain and problems? It's easy to do whenever we remain focused on our personal pain or insult. We close down, become hard, and choose the path of self-protection.

Following are some steps we can take toward positive conflict resolution:

1. *Focus on the one we love,* not the pain our spouse has caused us.
2. *Refuse to run away.* Staying focused on our lover requires us to stay planted side by side. We must reach out and touch the one from whom we want to separate. Staying "in touch" is essential to conflict resolution. Today we must decide we will not run and hide from each other or the problem.

3. *Remind ourselves of our only two choices:* to protect ourselves or to give ourselves to understanding the other.
4. *Look to God.* When we hurt and need to forgive our spouse, God will empower us if we ask. Sometimes we need to remember how undeserving we are of God's forgiveness in order to see the need to forgive our spouse's sin.
5. *Refuse to punish ourselves.* If we hold on to our hurt and pain, we may allow a root of bitterness to grow in our heart. The Bible says this can defile us (see Hebrews 12:15). The defilement may include anxiety, headaches, depression, and stomach and chest pain. We must learn to forgive and let go of the past, focusing instead on understanding more about the person we love.

FOR STRONGER, DEEPER COUPLE LIFE

1. What grade would you give yourself for remaining focused on the present in your marriage:
   • an A for refusing to ever bring up past hurts?
   • a B for bringing up past problems occasionally?
   • a C for bringing up old hurts monthly?
   • a D for living somewhat in the past?

2. Have you ever allowed a root of bitterness to grow in your heart because you refused to let go of past pain? Explain. Has it hurt you physically and/or mentally?
3. Do you, in general, have trouble letting go of past hurts? Why?
4. What positive change might you make in how you respond to your spouse when he or she has hurt you? End this session with a hug.

PUTTING CONFLICT RESOLUTION INTO PRACTICE

Do not let the sun go down while you are still angry,
and do not give the devil a foothold.
EPHESIANS 4:26-27

Challenge for the Week: Ask God to reveal to you any anger that has a foothold in your life. Pray, asking him to forgive you for focusing on the past. Then consider asking your spouse's forgiveness for spoiling today with yesterday's pain.

FORGIVENESS
Touches and Resolves

Iwas 20 and he was 26. We had been married two years and I hadn't dreamed he could be unfaithful. The awful truth was brought home to me when a young widow from a neighboring farm came to tell me she was carrying my husband's child. My world collapsed. I wanted to die. I fought the urge to kill her. And him.

"I knew that wasn't the answer. I prayed for strength and guidance. And it came. I knew I had to forgive this man, and I did. I forgave her too. I calmly told my husband what I had learned and the three of us worked out a solution together. . . . The baby was born in my home. Everyone thought I had given birth and that my neighbor was 'helping me.'. . . The little boy was raised as my own. He never knew the truth.

"I have never [again] mentioned this incident to my husband. It has been a closed chapter in our lives for 50 years. But I've read the love and gratitude in his eyes a thousand times."[8]

This woman *resolved* to forgive. She cared more about being rightly related than about being right, and that resolve led to her forgiving her husband and the woman with whom he had the affair. Forgiveness is a choice we make, not an emotion we feel.

Excellent forgiveness. What does it require of us?

1. *We resolve to pray.* The woman found the strength to forgive, not in herself, but in the Lord.
2. *We resolve to forgive.* The wife felt like murdering her husband and the other woman. She ignored her feelings, and with God's help and guidance, she forgave.
3. *We resolve not to think continually about a wrong inflicted,* rehashing the act and recalling the pain. We do not know how the brave woman in the story handled her mental pain, but we can imagine the battle she had to wage.

One great help is to practice "replacement thinking." In replacement thinking we decide in advance what we will think about—what we will replace the resentments with—when an old resentment reruns in our mind (we'll discuss this more later).

4. *We resolve not to bring up again our personal pain or the other's sin.* The generous forgiver in our story never messed up today with yesterday's pain.

Corrie ten Boom, a Dutch woman who spent years in a German concentration camp, reminded her worldwide audiences that God places our sins in the depths of the ocean "and posts a sign reading 'No fishing.'" She asked, "Can we do less for ourselves?"

5. *We resolve to forgive.* The wife accepted her husband as if he had never sinned and the baby as her own.

An excellent marriage requires two excellent forgivers. On a scale of

1 to 10, with 10 being a great forgiver and 1 being a grumpy grudgekeeper, how would you rate yourself?

FOR STRONGER, DEEPER COUPLE LIFE

1. Share with each other your responses to the woman's story of excellent forgiveness. What feelings and thoughts did it stir in you?
2. Which of the five components of forgiveness do you find most difficult? Which do you find easiest? Share your responses.
3. After you resolve to forgive your spouse, how successful are you in refusing to dwell on his or her wrong actions?
4. When we tell ourselves we won't think a certain thing again, we have just thought about that certain thing a second time. This is where replacement thinking helps: deciding in advance what we'll think about when an unwanted thought resurfaces in our minds. Have you used replacement thinking? Does it help? What replacements do you use?
5. What can you do to make it easier for your spouse to forgive you? Discuss.

PUTTING FORGIVENESS INTO PRACTICE

Bear with each other and forgive whatever
grievances you may have against one another.
Forgive as the Lord forgave you.
COLOSSIANS 3:13

Challenge for the Week: Whenever you catch yourself thinking about rehashing an old hurt, try replacement thinking. Some suggestions are singing a favorite song, meditating on a psalm or poem, or naming your spouse's good qualities.

EMOTIONAL INTIMACY
Opens Up and Speaks Candidly

E motional intimacy occurs when we speak candidly to one another about the emotions stirring our hearts and minds. Emotional intimacy speaks freely, understanding emotions to be neither right nor wrong, simply neutral. Emotional intimacy unveils the inner self, knowing our spouse will understand and not judge us for any feelings we have.

Why do we, all too often, play with our spouse the game of emotional hide-and-seek? Many times it's because we're afraid that we can't speak candidly.

1. We're afraid our emotions will make us look foolish. Since emotions are our initial, involuntary response to a situation or person, we cannot control their invasion of our life. And often our response to the same situation is far different from another's. This may cause us to fear that our reaction isn't "adult" or acceptable. This fear of appearing foolish to our spouse may keep us from sharing our differences with the other.

2. We fear because we refuse to recognize emotions as neutral,

neither right nor wrong, good nor bad, silly nor sensible. To the extent we accept the neutrality of emotions we will be set free to share with our spouse.

3. We feel helpless to control our emotions. We can work hard and succeed; but we may want to feel happy and not succeed.

4. We don't like how emotions leave us feeling. We may wish to feel warm and loving toward our spouse but end up feeling irritable and withdrawn. When this happens, we may judge ourselves to be somehow flawed.

Because emotions are difficult, it's tempting to build a thick inner wall of protection to shield us from feeling certain ones, or to bury our own uncontrollable emotions deep in the pit of our stomach. But there are two reasons to reject these options:

- *Reason #1:* Trying to pick the emotions we will feel is similar to a person's trying to eat only the sugar in a chocolate bar. In both attempts we must take all or none. When we guard ourselves against experiencing certain emotions, we risk losing all emotional responses. We risk becoming emotionally shut-down people, unable to experience the pain or joy of another.

- *Reason #2:* Buried emotions have a way of reappearing. As John Powell says, "When I repress my emotions my stomach keeps score."[9]

Being made in the image of God includes an individual emotional makeup. From Genesis to Revelation God speaks candidly about his emotions. He constantly reminds us of his love (Psalm 100:5), his jealousy (Exodus 20:5), his anger (Deuteronomy 32:19), and more. God owns up to his emotions, saying, "Yes, I feel that." Should we do less? Even negative emotions enrich our life and work for our good: Anger energizes us to fight evil; fear saves us from foolish mistakes such as jumping off a high cliff; depression may signal a need to shut down and rest. There is a positive side to every emotion.

There is also a positive reason to share candidly with our spouse what we are feeling: Hidden emotions control us. But emotions that are fully expressed and understood lose their power over our lives. If we share our emotions candidly with our spouse, we're set free to move beyond our emotions into greater intimacy in marriage.

FOR STRONGER, DEEPER COUPLE LIFE

1. Of the four fears listed, which might cause you to hide feelings from your spouse? Share your feelings with your spouse.
2. Have you ever hidden behind a wall of protection so you wouldn't have to feel certain emotions? Describe that time.
3. On a scale of 1 to 10 (with 1 being difficult to share and 10 being extra easy), how easy is it for you to share with your spouse your emotions? Explain your reasons to your spouse.
4. Did you feel more free or less free to share candidly when you were dating?
5. What things can you do together to introduce or return to greater emotional intimacy in your marriage?

PUTTING EMOTIONAL INTIMACY INTO PRACTICE

Therefore each of you must put off falsehood and speak truthfully to his neighbor [you are your spouse's closest neighbor], for we are all members of one body.
EPHESIANS 4:25

Challenge for the Week: Speak candidly with your spouse when you might normally remain silent about your thoughts or emotions.

PHYSICAL INTIMACY
Strokes and **Romances**

Romance not only lights a candle or brings home flowers, it builds a bridge of friendship, caring, and security for the reluctant spouse to cross into the arms of his or her eager lover.

Every marriage book seems based on the assumption that a woman must be in the mood for sex, while all it takes for a man to be ready for sex is to be in the room. Is it fair to portray such extreme disparities that shame the pursuing wife of the reluctant husband?

This letter, sent to Ann Landers from a retired woman, is as poignant as it is funny:

"For me, making love with my husband, 'Pete,' takes precedence over everything short of a major national emergency. For Pete, making love to me ranks in importance somewhere after washing the car and feeding the goldfish. It happens only when there is absolutely nothing else he could be doing.

"We NEVER plan to have sex. According to Pete, to plan sex is immoral. . . . Pete views acting sexy at any time before sundown as a threat to family values."[10]

For an opposing view on sexual desire, Smalley and Trent say, "Men tend to be like microwave ovens—instantly ready to be turned on at any time, day or night, and also ready to hurry through the cooking experience. The average woman, however, is more like a Crock-Pot. She needs to warm up to the sexual experience and savor the process, and the thing that warms her the most is a quality relationship."[11]

No matter who initiates sex, one thing remains true for both men and women: Romance is sexless and essential. Following the death of his wife, C. S. Lewis wrote, "For those few years, H. and I feasted on love, every mode of it—solemn and merry, romantic and realistic, sometimes as dramatic as a thunderstorm, sometimes as comfortable and unemphatic as putting on your soft slippers. No cranny of heart and body remained unsatisfied."[12]

Romance may be defined as "Attending to our beloved so that 'no cranny of heart and body remains unsatisfied.'" Here are some romance truisms to consider:

1. Romance is best expressed if one of us is willing to be inconvenienced to show the other how much we care. The author of *A Severe Mercy* writes, "To be in love is a kind of adoring that turns the lover away from self."[13] Try the following:
   - a surprise note in a lunch box to say "Last night was great!" or "Just wanted to say 'I love you'"
   - a special trip to a bonbon store across town to buy your spouse's favorite white chocolate, or to the farmer's market thirty minutes away to get your spouse's favorite white bread
   - an unexpected phone call to say "I miss you!" A thirty-second call from the kitchen, shop, or office is a guaranteed romancer.
   - arriving home with a long-stemmed red rose in hand. *Cau-*

tion: Don't limit buying flowers to the days you have sex. And don't limit wearing cologne or perfume to times of hoping for sex. Wear it every night!

- Be romantic for the only viable reason: to express your love and appreciation for the spouse God has given you.

2. Romance allows anticipation to build throughout the day. Light a candle at the breakfast table to let the other know you desire intimate time tonight. Lay a flower on your spouse's pillow before he or she arrives home from work to suggest a special evening is your desire. You may even want to try this small, inexpensive, romantic touch: turned down sheets and a chocolate candy on the pillow case.

3. Romance needs peace of mind and heart. Whenever anticipating lovemaking, keep the evening's conversation positive. The fact that your child brought home a disappointing report card can wait until tomorrow's breakfast. And, most important, refuse to belittle the one who forgot to pick up bread and milk!

4. Romance requires a relationship free of resentment, anger, pain, and hurt. Reject jumping in bed "to make up." Take time for healing first, so that the one who spoke harshly has the opportunity to communicate grief and sorrow over hurting the other. Romance keeps a soft, tender heart toward the other.

5. Romance invests time. Elongate every kiss with warm affection, beginning in the morning and repeated when back together after a day's work. Refuse to let your good-byes and greetings be nothing more than touch-and-go brushes. If you spend five seconds instead of a half-second kissing, you elevate a peck to a romantic smooch.

FOR STRONGER, DEEPER COUPLE LIFE

1. How do you feel about knowing in advance that "tonight's the night"? Are you willing to spend time during the day anticipat-

ing the night with erotic thoughts about your sweetheart? Discuss your feelings with your spouse.

2. Do the following exercise individually first. Then share your responses—and creative ideas—with your spouse! Which of these activities would you choose to plan for a perfectly romantic evening?
   - burn aromatic candles in the bedroom
   - create secret signals for "Let's make love tonight!"
   - take a bubble bath together by candlelight
   - shower together, caressing each other's body with liquid soap
   - spread out sleeping bags on the living room floor (or outside under the stars, if you live in a more rural neighborhood)
   - spray sheets with perfume, or use special sheets just for love-making
   - enjoy a candlelight dinner at a romantic restaurant
   - make a candlelight dinner for just the two of you at home
   - other (fill in your own ideas!) _____

Putting Romance into Practice

May your fountain be blessed, and may you
rejoice in the wife of your youth. A loving doe,
a graceful deer—may her breasts satisfy you always,
may you ever be captivated by her love.
PROVERBS 5:18-19

Challenge for the Week: Plan a twenty-four-hour getaway at home, minus kids. Each of you come up with eight details to make the night romantic—then do it!

SPIRITUAL LIFE
Blesses and **Reaches**

Why should we reach out to God in our marriage?

First, *we'll become closer in marriage.* There is a natural law that says, "When two objects are close to the same object, they of necessity are closer to each other." This is a spiritual law as well. The closer we get to God, the closer we'll be to one another. A double blessing!

Second, *we'll live a more fulfilled life.* The closer we get to God, the more meaning, significance, and satisfaction we'll find in living. As we grow more satisfied, we place fewer demands on one another—and that frees us to love our spouse more fully. Unless a spouse is spiritually fulfilled, he or she often insists that the other spouse meet the most basic needs of security and significance, two needs that God alone can fully meet.

Psychologist and author Larry Crabb defines our two deepest needs this way:

"Security: A convinced awareness of being unconditionally and totally loved without needing to change in order to win love, loved by a

love that is freely given, that cannot be earned and therefore cannot be lost.

"Significance: A realization that I am engaged in a responsibility or job that is truly important, whose results will not evaporate with time but will last through eternity, that fundamentally involves having a meaningful impact on another person, a job for which I am completely adequate."[14]

Crabb lists four possible ways of responding to these needs:

1. ignore our needs
2. find satisfaction in achievement
3. attempt to meet our needs in each other
4. depend on the Lord to meet our needs

The first may be the most dangerous because "when personal needs for security and significance are neglected and go unsatisfied, we move toward personal death. The symptoms . . . include feelings of worthlessness, despair, morbid fears, loss of motivation and energy, a turning to drugs or sex or alcohol to numb the pain of dying, and a sense of emptiness and boredom."[15]

The highest of mankind's achievements leave us dissatisfied. There is always a more successful person ahead. And our spouses? All are flawed at best and unable to fully meet our needs.

God's love alone never fails. His love never ceases, regardless of what we do or say. That's security! And God alone calls us into a life that will last throughout eternity. God invites us to become a member of his family—to work with him to establish his kingdom. That provides genuine significance!

Pascal, a philosopher and physicist, wrote, "There is a God-shaped vacuum in the heart of every man which cannot be satisfied by any created thing but only by God, the Creator, who is made known through Jesus Christ." Clearly, Pascal encourages us to look to God alone to fill our empty souls. No spouse is a sufficient substitute.

FOR STRONGER, DEEPER COUPLE LIFE

1. Do you agree that significance and security can be found only in God? Share your response with your spouse.
2. How aware are you of these two needs in your life right now? Give an example.
3. Which one of Crabb's four ways of responding to needs do you choose most often? Why? Do you feel completely satisfied with that choice?
4. Do you believe that God can supply all your needs? Discuss your responses together.
5. In what ways do you place on your spouse demands or expectations that he or she couldn't possibly fulfill? (Get your spouse's input on this question. Also, ask your spouse, "Do you ever feel inadequate or as if you want to run away because of my demands or expectations?")

PUTTING OUR SPIRITUAL LIFE INTO PRACTICE

My God will meet all your needs according
to his glorious riches in Christ Jesus.
PHILIPPIANS 4:19

Challenge for the Week: Reach out to God in prayer. Ask him to reveal himself to you.

LEVEL THREE

LOVE

Speaks, Discovers, and Acts

Awoman in counseling admitted, "I no longer have any feelings for my husband. I cannot touch him, and I don't want him to touch me. And you want me to reach out to him when I feel this way?"

"Exactly," the counselor responded. "The repeated positive action can have a positive effect on your feelings. Activate your love by your actions. Let us practice loving."[1]

Agape is the kind of giving love that marriages thrive on after the cooldown of erotic feelings. This love is something we do for the other's good, not for ourselves. It is an action of the will, a discipline we practice, something we give, not something we feel. Love is the servant of the will, not the slave of the emotions; love is an action deliberately chosen and directed toward another.

We need to remember four things about agape love:

1. *Love can be learned.* Just from working together on this book and reading other marriage books, we have found a new depth of intense desire for one another, a fresh thoughtfulness in our

marriage, and an increased unselfish attitude that asks, "May I help you?"

2. *Love acts on the other's behalf.* Love phones to see how it's going, selects a rose at the flower stand, helps with unassigned chores, runs errands. Little, unexpected things deliver a big bouquet of love.

3. *Love must be practiced.* Love can never be grabbed; it must be given. Love can never be demanded; it must be offered daily. Love does not come naturally; it must be practiced. Love practices giving compliments, offering encouragement, expressing approval, supplying elbow grease, expending time and energy, and meeting the smallest or most significant needs of each other.

In every marriage, spouses are challenged to present love to each other as a surprise package, wrapped in ribbons of thoughtfulness, kindness, and tenderness. Love is the only present that, when we give it away, leaves us with even more to give.

There's always an extra bonus of appreciation if we remember to do something the other has had trouble remembering or has been too exhausted to do: taking clothes to the cleaners, stopping by the post office to purchase needed stamps, filling a car with gas, cooking a favorite meal, cleaning up the kitchen when you're not on duty, offering to run errands or make phone calls for the busier spouse, etc.

4. *Love may be strengthened by habit.* Choosing and doing one thing daily for each other keeps love burning brightly in our hearts. As we search our memories for ways to delight each other, we stir up the warmhearted emotions of being in love. Planning surprises makes us even more eager to greet each other at the end of a day.

A wife writing to Ann Landers complained about her husband's lack of romantic attention: "When Johnny was courting me, I received roses, notes and phone calls. . . . We now have three children. There are no more notes, roses or midday phone calls. . . . I am totally in love with this man. . . . My romantic side, however, needs a booster shot. . . . All wives get a thrill out of receiving unexpected, inexpensive gifts and an occasional note on the pillow."[2] (By the way, husbands also get a thrill from extra attention.)

To be successful at surprises, we must study our spouse as we would study a work of art. We must learn our spouse's likes and dislikes, his or her favorite color, song, television show, ice cream, meal, dessert, sport, or hobby. If you don't know these things about your spouse, begin investigating so you can plan a surprise guaranteed to please.

FOR STRONGER, DEEPER COUPLE LIFE

1. Do you agree that love is an action you take, a discipline you learn, a habit you practice? Why or why not?
2. Do you think the woman who didn't want to touch her husband should get a divorce, based on a lack of feelings? Or should she try to seek reconciliation by continually acting in ways to best meet her husband's love needs? Why?
3. Refresh your memory of your primary love needs—and your spouse's primary love needs—by flipping back to Week 11.

PUTTING LOVING ACTS INTO PRACTICE

For God so loved the world that he gave
his one and only Son, that whoever believes in him shall
not perish but have eternal life.
JOHN 3:16

We know God's love by the actions he took on our behalf, not by the emotions he felt. Although he was brokenhearted about sending his only Son to die on the cross, he chose what was best for us.

Challenge for the Week: Remind yourself daily of your spouse's love needs. Plan three small actions to express your love, and carry out at least one of them in the next few days.

TOGETHERNESS

Gazes, Makes Time, and Plays

A common complaint among husbands is, "My wife won't do things with me."

When four hundred divorced men were surveyed, the reason virtually every man "cited as decisive to the failure of the relationship was the lack of companionship. Universally, these men felt that their marriages fell apart because they stopped being friends with their wives."[3]

Writer Carole Mayhall reports that when her husband, Jack, bought her a set of golf clubs, signed her up for lessons, and purchased a golf outfit, she decided he really wanted her to play with him: "Enjoying golf together has added fun and companionship to our marriage. . . . I don't want Jack to have his most enjoyable recreational moments in the company of anyone else, male or female."[4]

In *His Needs, Her Needs,* Willard Harley lists recreational companionship as the second most important male need (after sex). He believes so strongly in shared recreation that he insists the couples he counsels follow this rule: "If any recreational activity enjoyed by one spouse bothers the other spouse or cannot include the other spouse, it must be abandoned."

His reasons? "Some of my best feelings occur when I pursue a favorite recreational goal. If I share it with my wife, I will associate those good feelings with her, and as my love grows for her our marriage becomes strengthened. If I share these emotions with someone other than my wife, I will also associate those feelings with that other person. By doing this, I have lost many opportunities to develop love with my spouse and may even have begun to threaten our marriage."[5]

Following are mental snapshots of four couples who are working toward recreational togetherness:

Picture the most feminine of females, her face powdered with road dust, her brunette curls covered by a bulky black helmet. She clutches her husband's waist, bouncing behind him on his 1340 cc Road King Harley cycle. When she waves, you see raw fear blazing from her eyes. You know she's praying! (Because she joined her husband in his favorite Sunday activity, her husband decided to join her at church every Sunday before cycling.)

Picture a Virginia state amateur tennis champion, a real sports nut, laughing and holding hands with his wife as they wind their way through a flea market, searching out carnival and Depression glass bargains. He once considered leaving his wife because she was no fun. Instead, he became a self-educated authority on antique glass, and he now loves bargain hunting with her.

Picture a pretty, pert woman sobbing nonstop because she shot and killed a doe the first time she went hunting with her husband. That was the end of her hunting career, but since then she's racked up hundreds of hours mastering other sports her husband enjoys, including rollerblading, trout fishing, rock climbing, and spelunking.

Picture a woman who loves to weave, standing a bit behind her exuberant, expansive husband as he announces loud enough for all two hundred ears at a cocktail party to hear, "Isn't this a beauty! My hand-woven blazer. My wife wove the fabric!" This man partners with his wife by encouraging her, cheering her on, insisting she's good enough to launch a line of handwoven dresses. When she does, he outbeams her when he tells me her dresses are selling today for over a thousand dollars each.

Recreational togetherness touches all emotions and comes in endless varieties, all requiring participation by two. The main point is that we need to play together spontaneously, regularly, deliberately, and even a bit recklessly.

FOR STRONGER, DEEPER COUPLE LIFE

1. Do you agree with Dr. Harley's tough rule on recreational activities for couples he counsels? Why or why not?
2. Does either of you have a controversial recreational activity? If so, share that activity in love, explaining to your spouse why you feel it's controversial.
3. Do you consider your spouse your best friend? Share your responses.
4. Do you feel there is a recreational lack in your companionship? For the next three minutes, brainstorm about a list of at least fifteen recreational activities you might possibly enjoy doing together. Then star the top five activities you would enjoy doing most with your spouse.
5. When you have completed your list and starred your top choices, compare lists. Did any of your starred activities match? If so, this list gives you possible activities to pursue together. If not, make a new list—together!

PUTTING PLAY INTO PRACTICE

A cheerful heart does good like medicine.
PROVERBS 17:22, TLB

Challenge for the Week: If time permits, consider doing one fun thing together now, like making fudge, having a five-minute rough-and-tumble on the floor, perusing a scrapbook of your dating days, or playing a game of checkers, chess, or cards. (If not tonight, perhaps another day this week?)

ACCEPTANCE
Appreciates, Finds Good, and Lets Go

Many people enter marriage clutching a handful of strings, each one tied to a colorful balloon labeled with an expectation.

A man might enter marriage expecting his wife to cook as his mom did, to serve a hot meal at 6:00 P.M., to meet him at the door perfumed and anticipating the joy of lovemaking, to get excited when his hockey team wins, to welcome his old friends to the house, etc.

A woman might enter marriage expecting her husband to be as romantic as he was when they were dating, to keep her car shiny and the gas tank full, to bring her flowers weekly, to praise all her efforts at cooking, to compliment her looks daily, etc.

The problem with expectations is that the other seldom acts the way we expect. Without realizing it, we set ourselves up for disappointments, and disappointments lead to frustration, and frustration to anger. With expectations, one spouse battles anger while the other fights feelings of failure.

Spouses who attempt to control by expectations have "should" thinking.

My spouse should care about me, my marriage dreams should come true, my sexual needs should be met, I should be first in my spouse's life, etc.

Before you read farther, ask yourselves, "When it comes to our marriage, which one of us gives the most?"

If your marriage is healthy, you'll both think the other contributes more. If you think you give the most, you are probably heaping expectations on your spouse.

Expectations rob marriage of all the joy of giving. They create a "you owe me" mentality. Instead of asking what we can give, we demand that we be given what we see ourselves as having earned.

- "I married my spouse to make me happy. And if she doesn't, then I'll find a spouse who will."
- "After all I do for him, the least he can do is turn off the television and talk to me."
- "I have a right to respect around here."
- "When I cook a special meal for my husband, the least he can do is thank me."
- "As hard as I work for this family, I deserve a hassle-free evening to watch my football game."

These marriage-destroying attitudes are a one-way street to grumpiness. The one expecting or demanding a certain response from his or her spouse is always disappointed; the one failing to meet the other's expectations feels miserably inadequate, sometimes even drained of the will to live.

What do we do with unfulfilled expectations?

We practice letting go of them. Daily we ask God to reveal all the expectations we're holding on to. Instead of trying to force your spouse to grab the string attached to your expectation of the day, imagine letting go of the string as the balloon soars up and away to God.

Give up your expectations to God, for he alone can change you . . . and your spouse.

FOR STRONGER, DEEPER COUPLE LIFE

1. Do you place unreasonable expectations on your spouse? (Have your spouse also answer the question, "Do you feel I place unreasonable expectations on you?")
2. In what ways do you or your spouse pick up on expectations? Is it something that is stated continually? a look? a tone of voice?
3. Do you think expectations rob you of the joy of giving to each other? Are birthdays, anniversaries, or Christmas difficult for you because of an "expected" gift?
4. What can you do to remove your expectations or to keep them from becoming a burden to your spouse? Share your responses.
5. Letting go of expectations does not require that you let your dreams and wishes fly away too. So if time allows, complete this sentence by listing your fondest wishes and dreams for your marriage: "One year from now, I would like our marriage to be . . ." Share your responses.

PUTTING ACCEPTANCE INTO PRACTICE

Your attitude should be the same as that of
Christ Jesus: Who, being in very nature God, did not
consider equality with God something to be grasped,
but made himself nothing, taking the very nature of a
servant, being made in human likeness.
PHILIPPIANS 2:5-7

Challenge for the Week: If an expectation of how your spouse should act resurfaces, tie a balloon to it and let that expectation soar off to God.

COMMITMENT

Wills, Teams Up, and Gives

Low good are we at *giving* to one another?
Is our love like a time-share: "I'll let you have my two weeks in San Diego if you give me your two weeks on St. Thomas?" That's fifty-fifty giving, often touted by secular marriage authorities, but insufficient for spouses seeking biblical oneness.

Some Christian counselors say our giving should be 100 percent to 100 percent: "I'll love and keep loving you with all my heart and will, without demanding an equal amount in return."

But agape, the unselfish, biblical love, demands 100 percent giving—period. Tim LaHaye says, "Marriage, under God, should be a one hundred percent to nothing proposition. That is, you should go into your marriage with the idea that you are going to give yourself for the purpose of making your partner happy and expect nothing in return. The result will be to make your partner happy. Of course, if you do that you will reap happiness in return."[6]

Following are five ways to attain 100-percent giving:

1. *We give without thought of receiving a payback.* If I fix your lunches the rest of my life, I won't require you to cook dinner once a month. If I take all the clothes to the cleaners, I won't expect you to pick them up.
2. *We give our emotional energy when we believe we have none left to share.* We always have a spare hug and two ears tuned to our spouse's emotional needs.
3. *We give our time when we want most to protect it for ourselves.*
4. *We give when unexpected.* For a long time, I wondered why I enjoyed giving to others all year, except at Christmas. Then I read a chapter titled "Gifting and Volunteering" from *As for Me and My House* by Walter Wangerin, Jr., and I knew why I disliked Christmas—because it arrives with a sleighload of expectations. I feel as if I'm expected to transform our home into a Christmas wonderland when decorating is not my skill; go caroling when I can't carry a tune; and buy gifts galore to please a long list of people when I'm insecure about my choices . . . and shopping rates minus zero on my list of fun things to do.

When a gift is expected, it's no fun giving it in marriage, either. Author Walter Wangerin, Jr., won my heart when he wrote about a totally unselfish way of giving unexpected gifts that he dubbed "gifting." For gifting to happen, the focus must be on the spouse, not the day or what the giving will give us in return: "A single rosebud . . . given uncharacteristically by a husband oblivious to the sweetness or sentiment of flowers . . . can melt his wife by the love expressed. This is a gift. He shaped it to her, not to his own instincts."[7]

5. *We give by volunteering.* Wangerin writes, "Volunteering makes a present of your self, in what you do—but didn't have to do and weren't asked to do—on your spouse's behalf. . . . True 'volunteering,' then, obeys no law, seeks no return, pays

no debt, plans no praise for yourself, nor proves your goodness—but purely, purely is meant to demonstrate by your time, your energy, and your action no more than this: 'I love you.' It's what you do, unbidden, unexpectedly."[8]

FOR STRONGER, DEEPER COUPLE LIFE

1. Do you feel you give more than your spouse does? If so, in what ways?
2. Do you feel your spouse gives more than you do? In what ways? Share your responses to these first two questions.
3. What is the difference between giving an expected gift and "gifting" or "volunteering," as defined by Wangerin?
4. Where are you in the process of 100-percent giving? If you want to work toward that 100 percent, what will your initial steps include?
5. Do you have more trouble giving your time, attention, or energy to marriage? Why?

PUTTING GIVING INTO PRACTICE

Freely you have received, freely give.
MATTHEW 10:8

It is more blessed to give than to receive.
ACTS 20:35

Challenge for the Week: Practice "gifting" or "volunteering" in at least one way.

COMMUNICATION

Listens, Questions, and Chooses

A talkative spouse daily verbalizes approximately 100,000 words. But much more important than the quantity is the quality of the words we speak to each other.

The Bible reminds us that, with our words, we possess the power to bring life or death to each other's spirit. The two questions for us as Christian spouses are: How effective are we at avoiding "communication killers"? and How effective are we at speaking "words of life" to each other?

Once we speak thoughtless and hurtful words, we can't recall them or erase our spouse's pain with flowers or candy. We don't eradicate the memory with a simple "Please forgive me." Painful words penetrate deeply into the soul. As Proverbs expresses it, "Reckless words pierce like a sword, but the tongue of the wise brings healing" (Proverbs 12:18). In contrast, as we read in Week 1, "Pleasant words are a honeycomb, sweet to the soul and healing to the bones" (Proverbs 16:24).

All too seldom do we stop and contemplate the powerful effect we have on each other's life simply by the words we choose to speak. Here are eight ways to kill communication:

- *Exploding.* We may erupt like Mount Vesuvius to terminate any conversation causing us discomfort.
- *Bible thumping.* We may use a Bible verse to pronounce the other guilty: "Well, if you don't forgive me, God won't forgive you."
- *The silent treatment.* We may refuse to say another word when we feel uncomfortably exposed.
- *The authorized version.* We may cut off meaningful discussion by assigning to our version of the story the same authority we assign to an authorized version of the Bible.
- *Weeping.* We may not be able to prevent a few tears from trickling down our cheeks, but we can avoid flash flooding the stream of significant conversation.
- *Judging.* We may pronounce the other guilty of stupidity, meanness, or thoughtlessness by saying, "That's the dumbest thing I ever heard."
- *Triggers.* We may trigger retaliation with sweeping generalizations: "We never do anything fun." "You care more about fishing than you do about me." "If you ever wanted to go anywhere except with the women from the office, I would faint."
- *Criticism/nagging.* Criticism or nagging only reminds the other repeatedly how he or she displeases us.

Instead of choosing the eight "communication killers" above, we may choose instead these eight "words of life":

1. *Express your awareness of the other's existence:* "Your eyes sparkle beautifully today!" "I love you in that sweater. Wow!"
2. *Admire:* "Your dinner was superb!"
3. *Appreciate:* "Our yard looks like we have a full-time gardener! I appreciate all your hours of yard work."

4. *Give thanks:* "Thanks for picking up the kids for me. The office was a zoo today."
5. *Encourage:* "You look so much thinner minus those five pounds. Keep up the good work."
6. *Acknowledge the other's emotions:* "You seem extra tired tonight, as if you're carrying a heavy load."
7. *Express forgiveness:* "Sweetheart, you know I forgive you. There's no need to bring up that incident again."
8. *Compliment each other in front of others:* "Did you know my honey won salesperson of the year?" A compliment spoken in front of others earns twice the appreciation.

FOR STRONGER, DEEPER COUPLE LIFE

1. Which of the communication killers have you used?
2. Ask your spouse the following questions:
   • Which communication killers do you feel I use?
   • Which ones would you most like me to work on not doing?
   • Of the eight listed words of life, which two would you encourage me to practice?

PUTTING COMMUNICATION INTO PRACTICE

The tongue has the power of life and death.
PROVERBS 18:21

Challenge for the Week: Consider saying to yourself daily, "The tongue has the power of life and death" as a reminder of the powerful influence you are on your spouse's life by the words you choose to speak.

CONFLICT RESOLUTION
Chooses, Focuses, and Replaces

Conflict resolution resembles walking through a mine-field of contact explosives. It's easy to detonate a conversation killer, but it's certainly not necessary if we tread cautiously. There is a way to avoid explosive conversation: by replacing "you" messages that blame with "I" messages that explain.

One author explains a "you" message as "any message that conveys the idea that I am the normal one, I am right, and you are abnormal, defective, or wrong."[9]

Sentences that blame turn conflict into a war zone, one of us handing the other an engraved invitation to fight:

- "You never care about anyone but yourself."
- "You always forget to let out the dog."
- "You put your parents before me."
- "You left the clothes in the dryer—again!"
- "You would rather listen to Peter Jennings than talk to me."

- "You never have a decent meal on the table when I return from a long day's work."

A better way to communicate our disappointments, displeasures, and discontentments is to speak for ourselves, to own the problem, or to express our feelings with an "I" message.

When I say, "I feel angry when we miss the trash pickup," I own my angry emotions instead of unfairly blaming my spouse for causing me misery. I am responsible for my own responses to life: You cannot cause my emotions, and I cannot cause yours. Your words or actions may trigger me to spill negative emotions I've been accumulating for decades, but I am responsible for spilling those emotions.

Our emotions are as unique as our DNA. What makes you cry may make me laugh. We fight unfairly when one of us blames the other for the emotions we display.

One way to speak for ourselves is to say: "I feel _____ when you _____ because _____."

Example #1: If you want to detonate an explosion, try, "You left the stinking garbage here to smell up the whole house. Can't you remember anything except when to play golf!"

Instead of blowing up, the speaker chooses an emotion ("I feel angry"), identifies the reason ("when you forget to take out the trash"), and explains the emotion revealed ("because it's impossible for me to take it out with two toddlers underfoot").

Example #2: To detonate an explosion, try, "You don't give a darn about me and my feelings. You know I like a clean house, and you're too lazy to bend your waist to pick up one tiny toy."

Instead, the speaker chooses an emotion ("I feel let down"), identifies the reason ("when I come home to the confusion of a living room with toys and clothes strewn about and no signs of a dinner in sight"), and reveals the reason behind the emotion ("I feel as if I don't matter in your life, even though I know this isn't true").

When we blame each other instead of explaining our emotions, the problem we're trying to talk out becomes the hidden explosive in the minefield of unresolved conflicts. Regardless of our best efforts to tiptoe around the problem, it will explode with the lightest touch.

For conflict to move past the emotions to resolution, we must remember:

- We are not responsible for the other's happiness or sadness.
- We must own our emotions.
- We must speak for ourselves, using "I" messages that explain instead of "you" messages that blame.

FOR STRONGER, DEEPER COUPLE LIFE

Practice speaking for yourself by

- identifying a positive emotion that you've had in the past
- explaining your spouse's action that stimulated your emotion
- explaining why this action evokes such positive emotion in you

Here are two examples of the above exercise:

a. "I felt so totally loved that day you drove home early through the downpour to be with me when they announced a tornado watch. You went out of your way to say 'I care about you.' That's why it meant more than you'll ever know."

b. "I feel like the most loved man in the world when you greet me in the morning with a kiss, a cup of coffee, and my newspaper. I know how little time you have. And when you remember me: Wow!"

Now create your own positive memory by filling in the blanks: "I feel _____ when you _____ because _____." The only thing better than one happiness remembered is two! Continue creating positive memories if time permits.

PUTTING CONFLICT RESOLUTION INTO PRACTICE

It is to a man's honor to avoid strife,
but every fool is quick to quarrel.
PROVERBS 20:3

Challenge for the Week: Remember to replace "you" sentences that blame with "I" sentences that explain. This decision will prevent differences from escalating to marital conflicts.

FORGIVENESS
Touches, Resolves, and Restores

I need you to forgive me!"

Amazingly, these six short words possess the power to restore a broken relationship. They stand in stark contrast to the trivial twosome of forgiveness, "I'm sorry." The disparity between the two is great.

Children say "I'm sorry" as easily as "I'm hungry." And small wonder. To say "I'm sorry" is to expect the person you have wronged to reassure you that you're really okay, just as if you never did anything wrong.

Think of how flippantly we respond to "I'm sorry." We reassure with

- "Oh, that's okay."
- "Forget about it."
- "Nothing to it."
- "You're fine."
- "I'm okay" (when we often are not).

When we're guilty of hurting the other, it's a natural self-protection to transfer the problem of our separation onto our spouse and expect him or her to reassure us that we're okay. But is that where the burden should lie? The guilty person, the one who yelled the nasty words, threw the book across the room, or dredged up a diary of old wrongs, is the one who needs to stop and seek restoration, not exoneration.

If we expect the injured person to tell us that we are okay, that we are excused, that it wasn't that important, then we are seeking exoneration. In such times, we want to make up, bypass the problem, skip talking about it, and focus on clearing our name. This is when we use the trivial two words "I'm sorry."

Exoneration is external, while *restoration* is internal and centers on the damage done to our relationship by our thoughtlessness or sin. When we are the offender, we need to come to the other in humility and say something like "I was wrong. I've hurt you and our relationship, and I need you to forgive me. I can't go on without a right relationship with you."

"I need you to forgive me" is the responsible confession that restores a broken relationship. It is also the perfect replacement for the irresponsible "I'm sorry."

FOR STRONGER, DEEPER COUPLE LIFE

1. Check under the appropriate category (wife or husband) the statements that you feel are true:

Wife   Husband

_____   _____   *I say "I'm sorry" instead of asking for forgiveness.*

_____   _____   *I am faithful in asking you to forgive me.*

_____   _____   *I feel you always forgive me when I ask you.*

_____ _____ *I feel you forgive me even when I fail to ask you.*

_____ _____ *I wish you would ask me to forgive you more
often.*

_____ _____ *I wish we handled hurts more quickly.*

_____ _____ *I wish we cared more about our relationship
than about deciding who's right and who's
wrong.*

2. Of the first four statements, do you agree with the ones your
   spouse checked as true? If not, why not? Discuss your
   responses with your spouse.
3. Ask your spouse the following four questions about any of the
   last three "I wish" statements he or she checked:
   • Why do you wish this?
   • Do you think this is a pattern of our relationship, or do you
     have a specific incident in mind?
   • How would you like to see us handle forgiveness?
   • Has my overlooking or bypassing an offense left you
     wounded?
   • Do you feel I need to ask your forgiveness?

Caution: We are discussing wishes of the heart, not facts of the brain.
You may feel that you forgive quickly while your spouse feels just the
opposite. So please understand that you are exploring to understand, not
to establish guilt. Just because spouses feel neglected doesn't mean they
really are. It is their *perception* of the truth, not the truth. However, what
your spouse thinks and feels is vital to your understanding of each
other—and an improved marital relationship.

End your time together with a tender touch. Communicate to your spouse that he or she is more important to you than deciding who is or is not wrong.

PUTTING FORGIVENESS INTO PRACTICE

In your love you kept me from the pit of destruction; you
have put all my sins behind your back.
ISAIAH 38:17

Challenge for the Week: Is your relationship suffering from a lack of your confessing "I need you to forgive me"? Start replacing "I'm sorry" with "I need you to forgive me."

EMOTIONAL INTIMACY
Opens Up, Speaks Candidly, and **Hugs**

When we share a painful thought or reveal a raw emotion, we need two arms to hug us, not one mouth to advise us. Advice giving shuts off emotional intimacy, the same as capping a jar of peanuts says, "No more!"

It's painfully difficult for a fix-it husband to understand that he does not have to fix his wife's emotions as he repairs a leaking faucet. Neither spouse is responsible for causing or solving the other's emotional crises. Both spouses are responsible for providing understanding and sympathy. Nothing more. Nothing less. (For a refresher on emotions, see Week 18.)

After we moved into a large, two-family home in Pennsylvania, I (Bobbie) walked around for two years saying, "I hate this house!"

Myron's standard reply was "Honey, I'll buy you another house." He wanted to fix my emotional makeup so he would never again have to hear my pronouncement against the home he liked. But what he accomplished, rather, was to agitate me and prompt repeated tirades.

Finally a friend refused to let my negative pronouncements turn her away. After listening, she asked a question instead of giving advice: "What is it about this house that makes you so unhappy?"

I was stunned. No one had ever asked me that. Everyone else had tried to shut off my negative talk because of their discomfort and dislike of my words.

This friend's wonderful listening helped me move beyond anger to discover what the real problems were. The lack of privacy living in a two-family house, the difficulty of entertaining guests without a presentable bedroom, the dirt of a coal furnace, and making every decision affecting our home with two other adults left me stressed, depressed, and exhausted.

After talking with my friend, I focused on tackling identified problems that could be helped and asked the Lord for patience to live with the things I couldn't change. I also cut down my negative proclamations from more than twenty-four to less than two a year.

If Myron had realized I was speaking from my emotions rather than from my intellect, my negative proclamations could have ended months earlier. I was pleading aloud, in the only way I knew how, for someone to understand my pain and frustration in moving from a four-bedroom, three-bath house to half a house with two bedrooms and one bath.

Unless my wise friend had listened carefully enough to realize I was asking for understanding, not advice, I might have continued my litany until Myron and I left Pennsylvania and returned home to Richmond, Virginia, twelve years later.

What can we learn about emotional intimacy from my story?

1. *An expressed negative emotion begs for a touch.* When we hear our spouse express hate, worry, fear, anger, anxiety, or depression, it's time to reach out and hug for a full minute when we feel most like running.

2. *An expressed negative emotion longs to be accepted.* To do this, simply open your mouth and say, "Aw," "Mmm," or "Ohh," as you continue to hug.

3. *An expressed negative emotion needs to be defused, not corrected, criticized, judged, or advised.* Close your mouth against dispensing any advice as you continue to hug.

4. *An expressed negative emotion (except your own) may leave you feeling helpless, uneasy, or frustrated.* But don't let your discomfort trigger advice giving. Continue to hug.

5. *An expressed negative emotion from our spouse is an invitation for us to slow down, sit down, and feel our spouse's pain, concern, or anxiety.* This usually takes about five minutes as you continue to hug.

6. *An expressed negative emotion begs for understanding.* "I'm sorry, so sorry you feel that way" clearly expresses understanding as you continue to hug.

7. *An expressed negative emotion yields to gentle questioning once it is validated and understood.* The questioning helps your spouse move beyond the surface problem to the underlying problem.

Remember H.U.G.S. when you hear any negative emotion from your spouse:

Hug
Understand
Gently question
Shun advice giving

FOR STRONGER, DEEPER COUPLE LIFE

Share with your spouse one of your biggest disappointments in life, emphasizing how you felt, not what you did in response. (A current one is best because it will give your spouse practical experience in not giving advice!)

PUTTING H.U.G.S. INTO PRACTICE

*Let your conversation be always full of grace, seasoned
with salt, so that you may know how to answer everyone.*
COLOSSIANS 4:6

Challenge for the Week: Practice using H.U.G.S. every time your spouse expresses a negative emotion. You'll be surprised how the emotional climate of your home can change!

PHYSICAL INTIMACY
Strokes, Romances, and Excites

The day I wrote this chapter, Myron had left early to run errands. I settled in to read the Song of Songs, the Bible's sensual story of married love. When Myron rushed back home to catch a television program, he was momentarily caught off guard with the intensity and passion of my 11:30 A.M. welcome home. He missed his show that day.

If you are missing some physical excitement in your marriage, we encourage you to read together (or alone) the most sensual book in the Bible, the Song of Songs. Usually spiritualized by scholars who say it symbolizes Jesus (the bridegroom) and the church (his bride), this book will give you a fresh look at married, sexual love.

As one commentary expressed it, "Of all the many books on marriage that are available in secular as well as Christian bookstores, none of them can possibly improve on the biblical teaching found in the Song of Songs. Here is romantic love for married couples that exceeds our greatest dreams and expectations. Here is a manual on sex that beats all secular viewpoints on how a man and a woman should make love. Here is the viewpoint of God Himself."[10]

We forget sometimes that sex is God's idea. It is not some defiled act that God tolerates; it is something beautiful he created and insists that married couples enjoy (1 Corinthians 7:2-9).

One stumbling block for Christian women's sexual arousal may be the belief that mental fantasizing and sexual thoughts are wrong, perhaps even lustful. (And they are, except with your husband.)

For most of my married life I blocked or quickly replaced all sensual thinking with my planned activities of the day. I just didn't feel comfortable owning any sexual thoughts. Now I don't want to offend God by refusing his good gift of sex. I encourage women to allow sensual thoughts about their spouse to build all day as they anticipate becoming one with him. Think about how good it will be to feel his kisses on your body. If you're at home for the day, draw a big tub of soothing warm water, add bubbles, and relax (or do this together when you get home from work).

A great way to prepare for sex is to read together a chapter from the Song of Songs each night for eight nights. Or read a chapter a night from David and Carole Hocking's *Romantic Lovers*. This book thoroughly studies the Song of Songs and explains the ancient imagery to help us better understand the romance of Solomon's and Abishag's words.

Increased openness, intimacy, and sexual freedom await you. Read the Song of Songs daily until you long for the sensual sex enjoyed by Solomon and Abishag and planned by God for us.

FOR STRONGER, DEEPER COUPLE LIFE

Take turns reading aloud the following passage:

How beautiful your sandaled feet, O prince's daughter!
Your graceful legs are like jewels, the work of a craftsman's
hands. Your navel is a rounded goblet that never lacks
blended wine. Your waist is a mound of wheat encircled by

*lilies. Your breasts are like two fawns, twins of a gazelle.
Your neck is like an ivory tower. Your eyes are the pools of
Heshbon by the gate of Bath Rabbim. Your nose is like the
tower of Lebanon looking toward Damascus. Your head
crowns you like Mount Carmel. Your hair is like royal
tapestry; the king is held captive by its tresses. How
beautiful you are and how pleasing, O love, with your
delights! Your stature is like that of the palm, and your
breasts like clusters of fruit. I said, "I will climb the palm
tree; I will take hold of its fruit." May your breasts be like
the clusters of the vine, the fragrance of your breath like
apples, and your mouth like the best wine.*
SONG OF SONGS 7:1-9

The scene in chapter 7 of the Song of Songs "is the private bedchamber of Solomon and Abishag. She has removed her clothes and is dancing sensuously in front of her lover and husband. The moment is special, romantic, sensual, intimate, private, but needed.

"Solomon is entranced by the movements of her dance. He starts at her feet and moves slowly up the body, ending with her hair. . . . (In verse two he describes her navel as a rounded goblet which never lacks blended wine.) . . . The 'rounded goblet' is referring to a bowl-shaped glass pictured as a half moon. . . . The fact that it contains mixed, spiced, or blended wine makes it a symbol of sexual pleasures . . . and tends to confirm the idea that her sexual organs are being described.

"One thing should be clear from this sensuous description: No part of our body is to be considered unattractive or off-limits within the bond of marriage. The Bible approves of sexual pleasure and enjoyment, and describes physical intimacy between husband and wife with no reservation or inhibition. . . . Solomon continues to move up her body. He pauses at her waist. . . . He is not describing the imaginary line above the hips. . . . He is referring to the lower abdomen, immediately above the female genitals, and pictures it as being beautiful, graceful, tender, and

119

soft. . . . [Solomon] loved to hold [her breasts]. . . . He enjoyed feeling them, but he did it gently and lovingly."[11]

1. Share with each other how you respond to the sensuality of the Song of Songs. Do you feel uncomfortable, surprised, shocked, aroused?
2. Do you allow yourself to think sensual thoughts about your spouse in anticipation of intercourse?
3. On a scale of 1 to 10 (with 10 being perfect) how much do you enjoy sex with your spouse? If your answer is six or below, you may want to read together one of the following Christian sex classics to gain new ideas and helpful suggestions to return romantic love to your relationship:
   • *Intended for Pleasure,* by Ed Wheat, M.D., and Gaye Wheat (Grand Rapids: Fleming H. Revell Co., 1977).
   • *The Gift of Sex,* by Clifford and Joyce Penner (Waco, Tex.: Word, Inc., 1981).
   • *The Act of Marriage,* by Tim and Beverly LaHaye (Grand Rapids: Zondervan Publishing House, 1976).

PUTTING PHYSICAL EXCITEMENT INTO PRACTICE

Set me as a seal upon your heart, as a seal upon your arm; for love is strong as death, passion fierce as the grave. Its flashes are flashes of fire, a raging flame. Many waters cannot quench love, neither can floods drown it. If one offered for love all the wealth of his house, it would be utterly scorned.
SONG OF SONGS 8:6-7, NRSV

Challenge for the Week: Settle in bed together at least one night this week (maybe tonight), and reread the selected verses above or one chapter from the Song of Songs. Try it with the wife reading the Beloved's words and the husband the Lover's words. (Skip what the Friends have to say.)

SPIRITUAL LIFE
Blesses, Reaches, and Locates

Locating a good church home is like selecting ears of corn at a vegetable stand. We have to get past the shucks, the outer shell, to learn if the ear is mature, full, and fresh.

It doesn't matter if the farmer tells us he picked his corn two hours ago. If it doesn't seem fresh to us, we reject it. And it doesn't matter how much family members or friends rave about their church. We must invest the time required to discover for ourselves the church that will satisfy our spiritual hunger.

In locating a church home, we need to remember that we left home on the day of our marriage to cling to one another. God alone needs to guide us, and we alone have to be satisfied. In locating a church, we'll need good negotiating skills, like the ones we use in buying a home, choosing a Friday-night movie, or deciding where to spend our vacation. Remaining flexible, we must embrace the give-and-take of negotiation, remembering that *we never negotiate our faith in Jesus Christ, only the expression of it.*

William L. Coleman reminds us, "Too often Christians come from a background where compromise was a dirty word. We believed you did things because they were 'right' or because you were 'told to.' If all of life could be handled that way, then 'deals' wouldn't be necessary. But in the intimate world of marriage, smart couples either learn the word *concession* or they usually learn the word *misery.*"[12]

In this sinful world there is something wrong with every church because of the sinners, like us, who attend. But we may negotiate to find one where we'll discover the joy of worshiping together.

FOR STRONGER, DEEPER COUPLE LIFE

If you already have a church home, use the following exercise to learn how well this church meets your needs. If you are totally pleased with your church, use the following exercise to learn a new negotiating method that is transferable to any decision-making problem.

1. Read the following list of fourteen factors that would influence your decision of whether or not to go to a particular church. Brainstorm about any other possible factor you can think of, and add it to this list.
2. *Spouses should do the next part of this exercise separately:* Place a value from 1 to 10 on each of the fourteen descriptive statements, with 10 being very important to you, and 1 having little significance to you.

_____ *I want a church with a healthy balance of spiritual and social activities.* _____

_____ *I want a church with music that will draw me closer to God.* _____

_____ *I want a church that reaches out in local, national, and international missions.* _____

_____ *I want a liturgical church.*   _____

_____ *I want a church where I'll be challenged to grow, with*   _____
clear biblical applications to everyday living.

_____ *I want a church that is the right denomination.*   _____

_____ *I want a church that is friendly and outgoing.*   _____

_____ *I want a church where Jesus Christ is proclaimed as*   _____
Lord and Savior.

_____ *I want a church with an informal service.*   _____

_____ *I want a church that reaches out to meet the needs of*   _____
couples with special classes, retreats, etc.

_____ *I want a church that prays.*   _____

_____ *I want a church where the Bible is the basis for*   _____
teaching and sermons.

_____ *I want a church with a strong Sunday school program*   _____
for children and teens.

_____ *I want a church with an excellent nursery.*   _____

3. Combine both of your scores for each of the points, and
   circle the seven top descriptive statements.

4. Now mark the following statements with an *X:*
   a. Individually write an *X* by any of the seven descriptive
      statements that you consider nonnegotiable. Give that

statement 5 points for one *X* (listed as an *X* by one of you) and 10 points for two (listed as an *X* by both of you).

  b. Individually place a check mark by any of the top seven statements you find negotiable. Subtract 5 points for one check and 10 points for two.

  c. Repeat steps *(a)* and *(b)* with the seven descriptive statements not circled.

5. Star the top four point-getters. You now have your "all-star descriptive statements" to use in scoring each church you visit.

6. Together list all local churches you want to visit.

7. Visit each church two times.

8. Rate each church after the second visit. Using your "all-star descriptive statements" only, individually give each statement a 1 to 10 value. Add your four individual scores together.

9. Combine each of your scores, and you'll have the "total church score" to compare with other churches you visit.

10. After visiting all churches under consideration, choose the two highest-scoring churches, and visit each one for eight weeks. At the end of eight weeks, retest the church's score, using the "all-star descriptive statements." Visit the second church, retest, and compare final scores of your top two choices. The highest score is the winning church. You may consider attending this church four months longer to confirm your choice.

PUTTING OUR SPIRITUAL LIFE INTO PRACTICE

Let us not neglect our church meetings, as some people do.
HEBREWS 10:25, TLB

Challenge for the Week: Worship God, no matter where you go to church.

LEVEL FOUR

LOVE

Speaks, Discovers, Acts, and Encourages

Spouses may learn a lesson in encouragement from a professor in a small New England college. Early in his career, the professor decided to give every discouraged student a better mark than he or she deserved. Invariably, the next time around the discouraged student perked up and earned the same grade given when he or she least deserved it.[1]

Wouldn't it be great if, when we feel discouraged about life and ourselves, our spouse would encourage us by giving us a higher grade than deserved? If our spouse said, "I'm so glad you're my husband (wife). I wouldn't have anyone else," we would perk up and match or surpass the kind words spoken.

With affirmation as my number-one love need, I consider myself to be married to a number-ten encourager. Daily Myron bathes me in soothing, warm words of encouragement such as, "I love you," "I appreciate you," "You cook the best meals," "You work so hard for us."

The best way to encourage your spouse is frequently. God commands us to encourage one another daily (Hebrews 3:13). Why?

Author Gayle Roper answers this question when she explains the difference between praise and encouragement: "Praise is ever given to God. We don't call out encouragement to him. . . . He is the Ultimate Finished Product, and we offer him praise for who he is and what he has done.

"We, on the other hand, are rarely worthy of praise . . . the greater need of our lives is encouragement because the greater experience of our lives is skinned knees, stubbed toes and bruised hearts."[2]

We need to be cheerleaders for our spouses, calling out, "You can do it! You're super! Go for it!"

What does an encourager do?

1. *An encourager comforts, consoles, and takes the other's side:* "You must have felt terrible when that happened! I'm so sorry they turned down your proposal." (Never say, "If you had taken more time to write that proposal, it would have been accepted." We don't kick a spouse when he or she is down.)

2. *An encourager looks for things to admire in the other:* "You look handsome in blue!" "I love your smile (your jokes, singing, playing with the kids, cooking—whatever!)" (Never say, "That shirt calls attention to your fat neck.")

3. *An encourager lifts our spirits by pitching in to help with chores:* "Honey, let me help you fold the clothes," or "Why should you do all the lawn work? Move over. I'm coming out to rake leaves." (Never say, "I can't believe you've actually offered to help me.")

4. *An encourager surprises:* The encourager takes his or her spouse on a mystery date, buys a gift when it's not Christmas, calls just to say "I love you."

5. *An encourager expresses interest in the other's activities:* An encourager remembers to pray, phone, or inquire, "How did

your meeting with Mr. Turner go? I was praying. (Try to avoid
having to say, "Oh, you did tell me you had to meet with your
boss today, but I totally forgot.")

6. *An encourager writes unexpected notes of appreciation:*
"What a great lover I married!" "Just a note to let you know
you're my favorite chef!" "Wishing the greatest husband in
town a great day!"

7. *An encourager empathizes with the other's emotions:* "Honey,
you seem stressed out. I'm going to clean up the kitchen while
you rest." "You look exhausted. Here. Grab the newspaper for
a fifteen-minute rest before dinner. I'll bring the coffee."

8. *An encourager is there just for us.* Whenever we're in the lime-
light performing, the most encouraging moment is to look
across the audience and find our spouse beaming back at us!
When the other calls to say things aren't going too well, we
may want to show support by showing up for a surprise lunch.

FOR STRONGER, DEEPER COUPLE LIFE

1. How many of the eight listed "encouraging behaviors" do you
do? *6–8 is excellent; 5–7 is good; 4 or below, poor.*

2. Take turns asking each other the following questions:

   • Were you encouraged as a child at home? at school? at
   church?

   • Does encouragement come naturally to you, or is it a decision of your will? Explain.

   • Do you generally feel I encourage you? *If you are the
   answering spouse, remember to answer with love in your
   heart and kind but honest words on your lips.*

   • Are there some ways in which I might encourage you more?
   What would mean the most to you?

PUTTING ENCOURAGEMENT INTO PRACTICE

So encourage each other to build each other up,
just as you are already doing.
1 THESSALONIANS 5:11, TLB

Challenge for the Week: Be sure to encourage your spouse in one of the ways he or she said means the most.

TOGETHERNESS

Gazes, Makes Time, Plays, and Converses

Remember the long conversations you enjoyed when you were dating? André Maurois describes an excellent marriage as "a long conversation that always seems too short." But the opposite is true of many marriages.

When we go out to dinner, if we look around the restaurant, we may discover that a majority of couples are eating in silence, looking up from their food only long enough to gaze around the restaurant at others. These couples suffer from the sad malady of boredom. They've lost interest in one another. They can't think of anything to say.

If you were eating out together with your spouse and someone observed you, in what category would they place you: the bored or the bantering, the verbose or the very quiet, the turned off or the turned on?

In his book *Love Is a Decision*, Gary Smalley compares meaningful conversation to life-giving water. He writes about a photograph of a farmer who had waited more than a year for rain, "and now at last he had a chance. His face was turned up to the sky as the desperately needed rain poured down and mingled with his tears. . . . In a marriage, meaningful words are like those raindrops. They can bring life-giving water to the soil of a person's life. In fact, all loving and meaningful relationships need the continual intake of the water of communication, or they simply dry up."[3]

If our marriage is a bit dry around the edges, what can we do to return more meaningful conversation to our marriage? Here are nine suggestions:

1. *Look at each other to see who will laugh first.* If you have a good laugh, you'll relax and talk more readily.

2. *If you are eating out, tune out surrounding activity; if you are eating at home, turn off the television and radio.* It's all too easy to let the television spoon-feed us pablum in place of meaningful conversation.

3. *Keep a notecard in your purse or breast pocket listing concerns your spouse expresses during the week.* Check the list to ask one of those warmly welcomed follow-up questions. Because our lives are often overscheduled, we easily forget to ask how Aunt Mary's surgery went, what the boss reported at lunch, if the Rotary Club or Garden Club speaker was effective, what the doctor or dentist reported, etc.

4. *Jot down jokes on that same notecard.* Bring something funny to share whenever you're together. Laugh with your spouse about the things you've laughed at during the week with others.

5. *Enroll in a class together at church, the YMCA, or a community college.* Take notes in church and during any class, and then discuss them together later.

6. *Ask each other a thought-provoking question as a windup to time together.* Examples: If you could relive one day with me, which would it be? If you could do anything in the world with me, what would it be? What is your favorite way to spend time with me? Tell me about your greatest joy as a child, a teenager, a high schooler. How did you feel about college, playing sports, etc.? Tell me about your most hurtful child-

hood memory. Who was your best friend at age five, fifteen, and twenty? In what ways were these friends alike?

7. *Join a club together to meet new friends.* People add life to your interests and conversations.

8. *Converse about the future.* Remember how you used to talk when you were dating? A vision for tomorrow will stimulate interesting conversation today: "What do we want to do next year?" "How would we like next year to be different from this one?" "What is one goal we can adopt and work toward achieving?"

9. *Eat at a new place to stimulate your palate as well as your conversation.* We look in our local newspaper and eat at one of the recommended restaurants each month. We've relished discovering little "dives" with gourmet delights as well as down-home eateries dishing up fries and barbecue.

If one of you prides yourself on being a person of few words, it might help if you thought seriously about what one withdrawn person confessed: "After months of therapy with a Christian psychologist, I finally could admit that a secluded person like myself, who withdraws from others, might be self-centered and even lazy. My therapist showed me that communication is work and interaction tiring. It takes much effort to listen closely and then activate the brain to think through an intelligent and appropriate response. The Bible never condones a lifestyle of isolation or loneliness."[4]

Wouldn't it be grand if we considered our conversations as precious to us as rain to the farmer in the dust bowl?

FOR STRONGER, DEEPER COUPLE LIFE

One of you should answer all the following questions before the other does the same. Any time you have fully listened to your spouse's answer, feel free to question lovingly. Then set some goals together.

1. Do you ever consider conversation as work? How do you respond to the paragraph above describing the silent partner? Do you ever feel as if there should be more to talk about with your spouse? Is your failure to talk ever because you're over-stressed, overly tired, checked out, or even maybe selfish? Explain.
2. Does any fear of criticism affect what you don't say?
3. How do you do with followup on concerns your spouse shares? Your spouse should then share, lovingly, how he or she thinks you do on following up on his or her concerns. Together, look over the list of nine ways to stimulate more meaningful conversation. Which one could you try this week? next week?
4. If time permits, ask each other one of the thought-provoking questions listed in this chapter (number 6), or come up with one of your own.

PUTTING CONVERSATION INTO PRACTICE

*May the Lord make your love increase
and overflow for each other.*
1 THESSALONIANS 3:12

Challenge for the Week: If you've discovered some selfishness in yourself, ask the Lord and your spouse to forgive you. Make a daily effort to try to remember a bit of news, an event, or a joke to share at dinner.

ACCEPTANCE

Appreciates, Finds Good, Lets Go, and Stops Criticizing

Before writing this lesson, I asked Myron a surprise question: "When was the last time I criticized you?"

I waited, shifting weight from one foot to the other, expecting to hear what I didn't want to hear.

Finally, Myron looked up and said, "I can't remember, honey. I don't know when you last criticized me. It's been so long. Maybe a year?"

I was elated—and shocked—to hear of my success, especially after repeated daily offenses of criticizing Myron for forty-one married years. Fourteen to sixteen months previously, while doing research for this book, the following quotation by Ed Wheat had stopped me in my tracks and inspired me to stop criticizing my husband: "The truth about criticism is almost startling when fully grasped: criticism can actually be the death blow to love, intimacy, and all the good things you want to build in your marriage. . . . I do not recall when my wife and I last criticized each other. After years of edifying, we are not even conscious of personal flaws in the other because we are so caught up in the pleasure of living every day together."[5]

A marriage so pleasurable that we are not even aware of each other's personal flaws sounds unimaginable. But we must not only imagine it, we must work to make it happen. Wheat's words scared me into change. Why continue a practice guaranteed to destroy our love, intimacy, and everything good we want to see happen in our marriage?

We would like to share a story about a husband we counseled; unfortunately, he rejected our strong warnings about criticism. This pencil-slim man had a plump wife. They came to us for help. Whenever the wife ate ice cream, cake, pie, or chips, the husband would tell her, "Just look at you, stuffing your face. You ought to be ashamed. Why do you lie to me and tell me you want to lose weight?"

When asked if his warning worked, the wife said, "When he attacks me, I eat a second serving—just to make him mad." She heaved a heavy sigh, looked down at the floor over her bulging tummy, and cried, "I just wish he could accept me like I am. I think that would motivate me to change more than criticism."

Attacking, criticizing, and harping on another's shortcomings are counterproductive. Finally the skinny man divorced his wife, and she immediately enrolled in a weight-loss program.

If criticism worked, think how perfect we would all be!

Why, then, do we criticize? At the root of most criticism is an exaggerated sense of self-importance, pride that we know what's best for the other if he or she will only listen! When we put down the other, we usually feel superior. We tell ourselves, *I wouldn't dare do what he or she is doing!*

Somewhere we have gained the false notion that criticism changes people. It doesn't. In fact the very act we want to change is set in concrete by our criticism. Here's why:

1. *Criticism leaves the other feeling let down and drained of self-worth.* After being attacked by a spouse, the other is most likely to reach for something to help him or her feel better (such as food, alcohol, or sex outside marriage).

2. *Criticism inspires more criticism.* A critical spirit in one can produce retaliatory criticalness in the other. Soon the atmosphere of the home becomes polluted with negatives.
3. *Criticism may drain away our spouse's love for us and increase his or her resentment against us.*
4. *Criticism breaks the law of admiration:* "People are attracted to those who admire them and repelled by those who belittle or look down on them."[6]
5. *Criticism enrolls us in Satan's army, doing his work against the one we love.*

John Drescher writes, "If we want to help others become beautiful people, we should work at it through sincere praise and encouragements. Praise is the warmth and tenderness all of us need to change for the better."[7]

FOR STRONGER, DEEPER COUPLE LIFE

When you ask each other the following questions, use all your listening skills acquired up to now. Listen to understand, not to agree. You are not asking your spouse for an intellectual statement, but for an emotional report of what he or she feels. Make today your first day of refusing all criticism of one another!

1. On a scale of 1 to 10, with 10 being total acceptance and 1 being very little, how accepted do you feel by me? What causes you to choose this number? Have you felt this way most of our married life?

   Caution: Remember, listening requires one shut mouth and two open ears.

2. When was the last time I criticized you? How did it make you feel?

139

3. What things would you like me to stop criticizing about you?
4. Be sure to thank your spouse for his or her honesty (and a hug wouldn't hurt, either!).

PUTTING ACCEPTANCE INTO PRACTICE

You have no right to criticize your brother [spouse] or look down on him [her]. Remember, each of us will stand personally before the Judgment Seat of God. . . . So don't criticize each other anymore.
ROMANS 14:10, 13, TLB

Challenge for the Week: Decide today to stop criticizing your spouse. Ask your spouse to remind you gently and with a smile whenever you forget and start criticizing again.

COMMITMENT

Wills, Teams Up, Gives, and Disciplines

W hen I (Bobbie) was in my twenties and early thirties, before making Christ Lord of my life, I was disturbed by my habit of wondering how a handsome man walking down the street might be as a bed partner. Even after enthroning Jesus Christ as Lord, the habit continued to haunt me, especially when I tried to pray.

I cried out to God, "What can I do? I'm helpless. The more I try to stop thinking certain thoughts, the more intense the images become."

Slowly, by reading the Bible and Christian books and by talking with trusted friends, I learned how to keep my mind pure.

Our minds are a maze of contradictions. One minute we may be tempted to daydream about an affair, and the next we're planning a romantic getaway with our spouse. Our minds need the safety net of preplanned discipline.

Jesus recognized that sin begins in the mind and warned us: "You have heard that it was said, 'Do not commit adultery.' But I tell you that anyone who looks at a woman lustfully has already committed adultery with her in his heart" (Matthew 5:27-28).

The King James Version of Proverbs 23:7 shares the same concept: "As he [or she] thinketh in his [or her] heart, so is he [or she]." (The heart sometimes is used interchangeably in the Bible for the mind.)

Commitment disciplines the mind to keep it from dwelling on thoughts of life with another spouse. Divorce, separation, self-pity, and ill will against our spouse begin in the mind and end in court with broken lives and broken hearts.

The first suggestion of divorce begins with the lies we whisper to ourselves in the privacy of our mind, such as, *I deserve better than this,* or *I can't take being treated like this one day longer. I've done everything I could to make this marriage work.* It is our self-talk that determines our response to life and the resulting emotions we feel.

The Bible identifies a specific cure for a mind that likes to wander in a minefield of possible explosives: "Finally, brothers [spouses], whatever is true, whatever is noble, whatever is right, whatever is pure, whatever is lovely, whatever is admirable—if anything is excellent or praiseworthy—think about such things" (Philippians 4:8).

What can we do to keep our minds pure?

- *Avoid self-centered thinking: I keep thinking this over and over. I'll never get free. I'm so terrible. How could I be thinking this again?* We may think about a fantasized lover or divorce the rest of our life if we depend on our puny powers alone.
- *Look away from self to the Lord. Jesus! Help me! You win this victory for me!* Call out to Jesus one hundred times a day if need be. Let our weakness drive us to the Lord.
- *Label sinful thinking as sin.* Pray, *Father, I am sinning, lusting after another man (or woman). Forgive my sin.*
- *Use "preplanned discipline."* When a sinful thought disrupts our peace of mind, let it trigger our saying silently or out loud, "Father, I now choose to meditate on (the Lord's Prayer, the

Twenty-third Psalm, a poem, any Scripture passage, etc.)." Or decide in advance you'll pray for everyone at the office, church, or in your family.

Myron recommends what he calls proactive thinking. When he is tempted to see a woman as made up of sexual parts, he uses self-talk as a reminder of the spiritual worth of every person, saying, "This is a lovely person, a child of God, someone I need to respect in my mind."

Preplanned discipline works because we cannot think about two things simultaneously. This discipline will prove invaluable with all the mental struggles against infidelity that we may have to battle during marriage.

FOR STRONGER, DEEPER COUPLE LIFE

1. Discuss together which of the four steps to a pure mind you would find most difficult. Explain your response.
2. Admitting a sinful thought to our spouse will often wipe it off the slate of our mind. Dietrich Bonhoeffer said it best: "Sin wants to remain unknown. It shuns the light. In the darkness of the unexpressed it poisons the whole being of a person."[8] What fears would keep you from confessing to your spouse an ugly thought of which you want to be set free (fear of sounding foolish, fear of ridicule, fear of laughter, fear of its being repeated to others, fear of its being used against me, etc.)?
3. Are any of your fears unfounded?
4. Take a slice of intimacy (a thought your spouse would never know about unless you revealed it), and share it with your spouse.

Caution: When you are the "listening" spouse, express gratitude to the "talking" spouse for his or her honesty and trust in you. You must honor this trust by never using the revealed thought against your spouse and by never sharing it with anyone else. This will establish trust for future disclosures.

Putting Discipline into Practice

May the words of my mouth and the meditation
of my heart be pleasing in your sight, O Lord,
my Rock and my Redeemer.
PSALM 19:14

Challenge for the Week: Complete this sentence for your spouse: "I was just thinking . . ."

COMMUNICATION

Listens, Questions, Chooses, and Cares

Houston Oilers' starting tackle, David Williams, taught the nation what it meant to give a gift of time. On October 17, 1993, Williams skipped a key game to be with his wife after she gave birth to their son, Scot. He was docked $111,111—a game's pay.

Later, on a television talk show, the starting tackle held his wife's hand, embraced her with his eyes, and gave her an affectionate smile as he said he would do the same thing again, even if he was fined a million dollars: "She needed me, and I wanted to be with her." He noted that he had a contract with the Oilers, "but we have a lifetime commitment."

His sacrifice painted a billboard message for America: When we care, we give ourselves totally to the one who needs us, even when inconvenient or when we feel we don't have the time.

The gift of time says, "I'm here for you. Let's talk."

Time is life's great equalizer; we all have the same twenty-four hours a day to share freely, to give grudgingly, or sometimes, like a Scrooge, to withhold totally.

What happens to love when one of us asks for time to talk and the other ignores the request, refuses to talk, or promises to talk later and forgets? The one who withholds time may not enjoy his or her planned newspaper reading because of guilt feelings, while the other may feel rejected, sad, or unimportant. We become two losers instead of two lovers.

As the most important person in each other's life, we deserve the other's precious time, not the other's spare time. The caring of communication may mean putting dinner on simmer instead of serving it; turning off the television during the evening news; folding the newspaper when primed to read our favorite comic strip, etc.

Of course, either one of us may have to wait to talk until it suits the other. One of us may need to be more sensitive to the other's activity when asking for time to talk, while the other may need to stop being the watchdog of personal time. It is hoped that both will care enough to stop all activity for the sake of meeting the other's need for a listening ear and a sympathetic hug.

Is there any better way to show we care than with a gift of our time, especially when it's inconvenient?

FOR STRONGER, DEEPER COUPLE LIFE

1. Discuss together how you feel about Dave Williams's sacrifice of missing a football game in order to be with his wife. Does hearing about it make you uncomfortable, warm all over, angry, or what? Why?
2. When your spouse asks you for a gift of listening time, how do you usually respond: as a generous Mother Teresa, an unpredictable cat, or a stingy Scrooge? Why?
3. When your spouse asks for time to talk, do you feel like running and hiding because you think, *I'm going to get it,* or do you experience warm feelings in anticipation of the time?
4. How did you, as a couple, answer question three? If either of you feels like you want to run and hide when asked for time to talk, you need to add a second request to your vocabulary. If "I want

to talk" indicates a problem with an expected solution, then a second request should indicate a need for empathetic listening with emotional understanding, minus advice or judgments.

5. Choose one of the suggested signals from each list, or make up your own. Check which one you're going to use the next time you need to talk with your spouse.

A Request for Time to Solve Problems

_____ *I need to talk.*

_____ *I have a problem. Can we talk?*

_____ *We have a problem. Can we talk?*

_____ *(Create your own.)*

A Request for Listening to Understand

_____ *I need a heart with two ears.*

_____ *I need you to listen and hug me.*

_____ *I need an understanding moment.*

_____ *I need you to listen.*

_____ *(Create your own.)*

PUTTING CARING INTO PRACTICE

> *Finally, all of you, have unity of spirit, sympathy,*
> *love . . . a tender heart and a humble mind.*
> 1 PETER 3:8, RSV

Challenge for the Week: Practice unselfish listening. Decide to lay aside your plans for ten minutes a day to give focused listening to your spouse. You'll receive tons of appreciation.

147

CONFLICT RESOLUTION
Chooses, Focuses, Replaces, and **Requires**

A recent survey of fifty thousand women revealed that 52 percent of today's women and 39 percent of today's men flee to the sofa when fireworks fly in marriage.[9]

Because the fight/flight syndrome is all too common among spouses, couples must make five decisions prior to any angry storms threatening their marriage.

1. *I will never walk out, stomp out, or flee from my spouse's presence while in the midst of conflict, except by mutual agreement.* If we choose the road to increased understanding of ourselves and our spouse, in essence we promise to remain together, resolve every conflict, and learn in the process. The only exception would be if the fight gets too hot to handle and we mutually agree to separate and return minutes or hours later. A cooling-off period may be beneficial.

2. *I will discuss any and all subjects my spouse needs me to talk about.* The subject isn't touchy—we are! Sometimes a spouse

may feel superior when he or she refuses to say another word to an angry spouse. Such a spouse may even brag about being the family peacemaker, when in reality he or she is making war on the marriage. Clamming up cuts off meaningful conversation. If we refuse to talk, nothing gets settled, and the stalemate produces tension that robs every day of peace.

3. *I will refuse to place blame, even if my spouse initiated the conflict.* It's easier to place blame than it is to assume responsibility. (The "you always" and "you never" statements of Week 6 illustrate this.) But in a conflict, two people are responsible for solving it. The question of who ignited the conflict is unimportant.

4. *I refuse to make conflict a win-or-lose situation.* Our personal relationship is more than a question of who wins. With a forced solution, the winner most likely will lose the warm affection and respect of his or her spouse.

5. *I will not yield to keep the peace at any price.* Giving in to be the nice guy who wants to get along all the time destroys our goal of using conflict as a means to mature and grow.

FOR STRONGER, DEEPER COUPLE LIFE

1. Which of the five decisions would you find most difficult to keep? Why? What experiences in your childhood or of conflict resolution in your marriage make this decision difficult for you?

2. Which of the five decisions do you think would help you and your spouse the most with conflict resolution? Is there anything standing in the way of your making the needed decisions?

3. Describe times when you were in conflict with your spouse and

- felt you were the winner
- withdrew and refused to talk
- yielded for the sake of peace even though the conflict had not been solved
- compromised with your spouse about a disagreement
- worked through conflict together with your spouse and resolved your disagreement

4. What is your relationship style in dealing with conflict resolution? (Hint: For which items above did you find it easiest to come up with examples?)

PUTTING CONFLICT RESOLUTION INTO PRACTICE

*A fool gives full vent to his anger, but a
wise man keeps himself under control.*
PROVERBS 29:11

Challenge for the Week: Review the five decisions. Choose one you will keep whenever conflict arises between you and your spouse.

FORGIVENESS
Touches, Resolves, Restores, and *Absolves*

I forgive you!"

This terrific triplet is second in power only to "I love you!" The three words that absolve our spouse of guilt sound so simple, so intelligent, so loving and kind. Why then would we ever hesitate to speak them?

More often than not, three things challenge our decision to forgive:

1. *Our pride.* Only a humble person, aware of his or her own sinfulness, will forgive another sinner. To grant forgiveness is to give to the other what we desperately need ourselves. Horace Bushnell said, "Forgiveness is man's deepest need and highest achievement."

2. *Our sense of rightness.* If we remain self-righteous, insisting in our mind that "we would never do such a thing!" then we end up on the bench, passing judgment on the wrongness of our spouse's behavior. To forgive, we must step down from the bench and let go of all judgments.

3. *Our desire to punish.* We not only decide in our mind that our

153

spouse needs to be punished, we also want to choose the best way to inflict it! But to forgive is to give up our desire to punish.

Karen Burton Mains, in *The Key to a Loving Heart,* defines forgiveness as "being willing to bear the pain of another's misdeeds." This definition is enlarged by Alice and Robert Fryling, who write, "Forgiveness does not mean we pretend we are not hurt. It does not mean we never talk about our hurts. Forgiveness means that in obedience to the example of Jesus, we willingly bear the pain of that offense, asking God to help us and to heal the wound of the relationship. We will never be asked to bear greater pain than Jesus bore. And we will never be asked to forgive a sin that has not already been forgiven on the cross."[10]

Dean Ornish recalls a heart patient who admitted holding anger against "an army buddy for betraying him to the enemy in World War II. He felt completely justified in his anger—and he probably was. Yet his anger was not hurting the army 'buddy' at all, who in fact had been killed years earlier during the war. But it was hurting the patient quite a lot; just telling . . . the story caused him to have severe chest pains. In effect, the patient was giving away the power to make himself sick or well and, ultimately, to live or die, to a man whom he most despised—someone who had been dead for years." Ornish insists we forgive "not to be a 'good person,' not to get a gold star, not to go to heaven—but simply because it is in our self-interest to do so. It's pragmatic: by doing this, we can feel more free of stress, pain and disease."[11]

Life is so brief. Why should we mess up one more day with the past? To absolve each other of guilt requires tearing up old IOUs, looking each other directly in the eyes, and declaring, "I forgive you." Our forgiving one another is most of all a sound investment in our future health and happiness.

FOR STRONGER, DEEPER COUPLE LIFE

1. Do you ever feel that your forgiveness of your spouse is conditional? For example, do you disqualify your forgiveness in any of the following ways? Check which ones apply. Then share your responses with your spouse.

   _____ I forgive you, *but I'm sick and tired of forgiving the same thing over and over.*

   _____ I forgive you, *but don't ever provoke my anger in the same way again.*

   _____ I'll forgive you *this time.*

   _____ I'll forgive you *if you promise not to make the same mistake again.*

   _____ I forgive you, *but I won't ever forget what you did.*

   _____ I forgive you (fill in the blank with any other way of disclaiming forgiveness).

2. Do you ever feel that your spouse's forgiveness of you is conditional? For example, does he or she disqualify offered forgiveness in any of the following ways? Check which ones apply. Then share your responses with your spouse.

   _____ I forgive you, *but I'm sick and tired of forgiving the same thing over and over.*

   _____ I forgive you, *but don't ever provoke my anger in the same way again.*

   _____ I'll forgive you *this time.*

   _____ I'll forgive you *if you promise not to make the same mistake again.*

_____ I forgive you, *but I won't ever forget what you did.*

_____ I forgive you (fill in the blank with any other way of disclaiming forgiveness).

3. Is there anything in your past for which you feel your spouse has not forgiven you fully? If so, share that with your spouse.

Hints for the listening spouse: Promise to listen without defending yourself or getting angry. Instead, try to understand. If your spouse names an event for which he or she has never felt fully forgiven, this is not the time to try to convince him or her that you forgave weeks, months, or years ago. Your spouse is expressing an emotion to understand, not writing a fact sheet to proofread. Please thank your spouse for telling you about the pain he or she has felt, and then reach out and give a tender touch as you look your spouse in the eyes and say something like, "I forgive you for. . . . You stand absolved, guilt-free, and in my eyes as innocent as if you had never committed this offense against me." Seal your absolution with a kiss.

PUTTING FORGIVENESS INTO PRACTICE

> *God was reconciling the world to himself in Christ, not counting men's sins against them.*
> 2 CORINTHIANS 5:19

Challenge for the Week: Practice forgiving others at the moment they treat you unfairly. Quietly tell the Lord, "I forgive _____ for _____." If it's your spouse, look him or her in the eyes, touch, and say, "I forgive you."

EMOTIONAL INTIMACY

Opens Up, Speaks Candidly, Hugs, and Empathizes

Lovers' hearts cry out to be examined. As John Powell says, "It is true that my values, beliefs, and goals are more important than my feelings, but only when I tell you how I feel about my values, beliefs and goals will you be able to perceive my uniqueness. It is true that my love is more important than my feelings, but only when I share with you the many feelings that my love stirs in me will you be able to see my love as unique and unrepeatable. The diamond is the person, but the setting that brings out and illustrates all the facets of beauty is the feelings. Without the setting the diamond couldn't be seen and admired. Without the feelings, the person cannot be known."[12]

In marriage, we want our heartbeat checked and recorded, but our lover all too often acts as if he or she doesn't know how to use the stethoscope of love, the ears.

Empathy requires us to stop and listen long enough to participate fully in the other's emotions and ideas. The Bible instructs us to "rejoice with those who rejoice; mourn with those who mourn" (Romans 12:15): in other words, to have matching emotions. Take the required time to allow what the other feels to impact your heart and to penetrate your emotions.

The other day Myron was eating lunch at the table, and I was pacing the floor with a hot dog in hand. Myron had found a love passage from a book he wanted me to hear and consider using in our manuscript. I sat down beside him, laid aside my hot dog, reached for his hand, and focused my attention on him. When our brief encounter ended, we separated with a kiss, and I returned to my computer a different person. My heart was pounding. I felt dizzy with the exhilaration. I felt as if I had climbed Mount Everest and was viewing life from the highest peak.

Excitedly I turned to my author "friend" John Powell, whose writing first convicted me of the importance of emotions. Although I had read *The Secret of Staying in Love* repeatedly over the years, it was on December 5, 1994, that I savored a peak experience and found it described in Powell's words on page 80: "Without these moments of breakthrough into new and mutual transparency, love becomes dull, stagnant and boring . . . In the garden of humanity what is not growing is dying."

How easily we bypass the peak experiences of life, seldom stopping long enough to hear the heart of a request.

The wife eagerly suggests, "The weekend weather sounds great. Let's plan a picnic in the park tomorrow and some bicycling."

"You gotta be kidding," the husband chides. "With all the work I have to do around this place? No way!"

Or the husband suggests, "Let's catch the baseball game tonight at the stadium. I need some fun in my life!"

The spouse replies, "That's not my idea of fun. Let's catch the early show instead."

These spouses were probably touchy and grumpy the remainder of the day. Why? Because rejection of our ideas feels an awful lot like rejection of us. And to be cut off abruptly is even more hurtful. How much better to practice the "stop and go" of genuine empathy!

Empathy is all about caring enough to *stop* and affirm our spouse by considering his or her ideas important enough to discuss, not dismiss:

"That's a great idea, honey. Let's talk about it," or "It sounds like going to the ball game is really important to you." Try using the three-question technique introduced in Week 15 to see why this idea means so much to your spouse.

Then . . . *go* for understanding. An understanding spouse would have cared as much about the feelings behind the request as he or she did about the request. A lover would have learned whether his wife wanted a picnic and bicycling to gain his undivided attention, to find relief from her tension, to get a good, physical workout, or to romance under the trees on a blanket.

The husband who needed a little fun in his life might have felt discouraged, overstressed from overtime, or in need of experiencing again the joy of having his spouse beside him at a baseball game.

This prayer of Francis of Assisi is born of unselfishness: "Lord! Grant that I may seek more to understand than to be understood."

"[Paul] Tournier feels so strongly about the need for understanding one another that he says the husband and wife should become preoccupied with it—lost in it—engrossed to the fullest in learning what makes the other one tick, what the other one likes, dislikes, fears, worries about, dreams of, believes in and why he or she feels this way."[13]

How do we get down to the emotions underneath the request? It will happen when you care more about understanding this marvelous spouse God has gifted you with than you care about being understood by him or her. *Stop* and put all your body energy into being fully present, and then *go* for understanding, making full use of reflective sentences ("You sound really hurt," "I'll bet that was embarrassing," "You've had a difficult time," or "I'm so sorry to hear how sad you are") and perception checks ("You sound really angry," "You must be terribly worried," "Am I right in sensing your fear?" "Do I hear you saying you felt deserted by your family?").

FOR STRONGER, DEEPER COUPLE LIFE

Take turns describing your time of greatest pain and then your time of greatest joy. When you are the listening spouse, practice the "stop and go" of empathetic listening.

PUTTING EMPATHY INTO PRACTICE

> *Clothe yourselves therefore . . . [by putting on behavior marked by] tenderhearted pity and mercy, kind feeling, a lowly opinion of yourselves, gentle ways [and] patience—which is tireless, long-suffering and has the power to endure whatever comes, with good temper.*
> COLOSSIANS 3:12, AMP

Challenge for the Week: If your spouse has plans, joys, or heartaches to share, *stop* and listen and *go* for understanding.

PHYSICAL INTIMACY

Strokes, Romances, Excites, and **Communicates**

Sexual bliss may be diminished by silence; sexual pleasure may be restricted by shame. But this is not how God planned it. God intended intercourse for pleasure. And that pleasure is enhanced by verbal communication. "Expressing positive messages during sex enhances the experience for both spouses," according to Cliff and Joyce Penner. "The one who expresses the moans and delights is releasing sexual energy. The one hearing those responses is aroused and encouraged in his or her enjoyment by that feedback."[14]

Walter Wangerin, Jr., encourages couples to communicate before, during, and after sex. He asks, "Why would you not praise her, thank him, for a gift well given? Or is the gift so unimportant that it merits no mention? Praising will preserve it, that it may become a part of your sexuality. . . .

"Talk unashamedly. There is no law to keep you silent about your bodies, about the sexual motions in them, all the sensations that come before a climax, the climax itself. . . . One of the holiest joys of lovemaking is the *spiritual* entrance into another human being—to know what someone else of the other sex feels like on the inside. . . . An expressive lovemaking truly draws us inside each other. Your spouse (if you talk!) can know your body *and* your heart."[15]

For the first years of our married life, we never talked about sex during our lovemaking (and we seldom talked before or after). During those silent years I communicated strictly by body language that Myron read well. But today we know the joy of communicating before, during, and after intercourse, and we savor the enhancement talking adds to sexual intimacy.

Now we talk openly during the day about our need for sex ("Let's go to bed early tonight and make love"). We talk freely about the kind of sex we'll enjoy ("This one will be a 'quickie' just for you"). We talk during lovemaking ("Caress here") and afterward ("Wow! You were magnificent!").

How is your communication before, during, and after lovemaking? Have you allowed silence or shame to rob you of maximum sexual enjoyment? If so, the time to talk is now.

FOR STRONGER, DEEPER COUPLE LIFE

Take turns reading aloud the following seven quotations, pausing after each reading for both of you to answer the following two questions:

1. What emotions, thoughts, and ideas does this quotation stimulate in me?
2. How does this quotation help me better understand our sexual successes or problems?

QUOTATION 1 "Take time to teach each other effective sexual stimulation. . . . Tell your husband (wife) what works for you sexually."[16]

QUOTATION 2 "Trust allows him, encourages her, to be naked before you and not ashamed. Naked physically: No part of the body is hidden since no curve of it, no organ or flesh of it will be hurt or troubled by embarrassment. Naked emotionally and spiritually: No part of the personality, no feeling, no memory or fear or internal delight need be hidden either, since *nothing* of your spouse will be hurt or abused or embarrassed. Trust allows him, encourages her, to present a whole self before you. And honesty in you, likewise, hides nothing of your whole self from your spouse."[17]

QUOTATION 3 "Both partners have to settle for human foibles and faults, and irritability and fatigue and occasional nighttime headaches."[18]

QUOTATION 4 "Your sexual relationship will always mirror the larger context of your life, revealing personal fears and tensions, and almost always serving as a barometer of the total relationship between you and your partner."[19]

QUOTATION 5 "The better alternative to selfish demands is thoughtful requests. I recommend these 3 essential steps: Explain what you would like and ask how your spouse would feel fulfilling your requests; if your spouse indicates that the request will be unpleasant to fulfill, withdraw the request; discuss alternative ways that your spouse could help you and feel good about it."[20]

QUOTATION 6 "Most sexual problems in marriage have little to do with physical technique but everything to do with meeting emotional needs."[21]

QUOTATION 7 "To prepare for sex by undressing and jumping into bed is to prepare *only* the body. . . . The sexual connection means you understand that you make love to a person, not a body."[22]

PUTTING PHYSICAL INTIMACY INTO PRACTICE

The man and his wife were both naked,
and they felt no shame.
GENESIS 2:25

Challenge for the Week: Before you enjoy your next sexual union (how about tonight?), share two things you appreciate about your spouse's lovemaking and one thing that would bring you more sexual satisfaction.

SPIRITUAL LIFE

Blesses, Reaches, Locates, and Grows

Join the following two sayings, and you have capsulized the secrets of Christian growth:

1. To grow tall spiritually, a man must first kneel.
2. The Christian who is careless in Bible reading is careless in Christian living.

Like two indelible ink pens, prayer and Bible study mark our lives for all eternity. To pray is to relate with the God of the universe, to enjoy his fellowship. To read the Bible is to allow God's timeless words to speak afresh to us as they have to mankind for thousands of years.

The Bible is as current as today's newspaper. It has been said, "I have read many books, but the Bible reads me."

Failing to read the Bible is like buying a new car and throwing away the owner's manual. Our car may end up in the repair shop twice as often as it should. In the same way, our marriage may end up in counseling or

165

divorce court because we refuse the wisdom of the one who invented marriage.

If spiritual life is new to you, consider the following:

- Begin your Bible reading with a modern translation in conversational English.
- Daily read one chapter from the Gospel of John. For variety, add a psalm or proverb a day.
- As you read, expect God to speak to you. Discuss your concerns with him.
- Incorporate God's corrections and directions into your life.

Just as foolish as discarding our owner's manual, the Bible, is neglecting prayer. The medical community has documented the importance of prayer to an extent that Larry Dossey, M.D., suggests, "Physicians who don't pray for their patients are guilty of spiritual malpractice. Experiments with people showed that prayer positively affected high blood pressure, wounds, heart attacks, headaches and anxiety. Those who prayed for family members or friends were also able to speed their loved ones back to good health. The effects of prayer did not depend on whether the praying person was present or far away. . . . Nothing seemed capable of stopping or blocking prayer."[23]

The power of prayer and Bible study is also documented by the lives of millions of Christians. But how are these spiritual disciplines to be enjoyed: privately, or as a couple?

Most Christians find it easier to develop a personal devotional life before establishing couple devotions. But the reverse may be true for you! Although praying together is delightfully intimate, many mature Christian couples find themselves feeling too uncomfortable to enjoy the intimacy. So where do you start in having personal devotions? You may find one of the following six suggestions helpful:

1. Try a five-minute, daily devotion you will faithfully observe for two months. If this habit has enriched your life and marriage, make a second, longer commitment of time with the Lord.
2. Consider mornings. The best way to start the day is with the Lord. Spending lunch with the Lord or nightly devotions work well. But whatever time you choose, remain faithful.
3. Read one chapter in the Gospel of John, a comfortable, warm book relating God's love for you through Jesus Christ, his Son.
4. After reading, listen for what God wants to say to you.
5. Consider praying the ACTS way: Adoration, Confession, Thanksgiving, Supplication. Praise God for his goodness; confess your sins; thank him for all he's done for you; ask him for what you need, and ask him to heal and help others.
6. You may prefer to use a daily devotional book. Many are available in Christian bookstores.

If you are eager to begin having devotions with your spouse, try one or more of the following eight suggestions:

1. After turning out the lights, hold hands and thank the Lord for his blessings of the day.
2. Offer brief prayers of protection for each family member at breakfast.
3. Memorize the same Bible verse weekly and share what it means to you.
4. Each morning pray the Lord's Prayer together.
5. On awakening have your first cup of coffee or tea, read the Bible separately, pray separately, and then pray together for family members.
6. Make spiritual sharing a part of your dinner conversation, with each family member sharing his or her greatest blessing of the day.

7. Play a Christian teaching tape and discuss it.
8. When traveling in the car, turn off the radio and pray for your biggest family concern.

FOR STRONGER, DEEPER COUPLE LIFE

Share your responses to the following questions:

1. What has prayer meant in your life up to now? How about the Bible? Has this week's lesson changed your thinking in any way? If so, how?
2. Do you have a personal relationship with Jesus Christ? If you are interested in becoming one of God's children, pray this simple prayer: Lord Jesus, I need you. I believe you died for me, and I receive you as my Savior and Lord. Thank you for forgiving my sin and giving me eternal life with you. Amen.
3. Of the eight suggestions on growing together spiritually, which two would you like to practice with your spouse? Why?

PUTTING OUR SPIRITUAL LIFE INTO PRACTICE

All Scripture is God-breathed and is useful for teaching, rebuking, correcting and training in righteousness.
2 TIMOTHY 3:16

Challenge for the Week: Choose one way to grow together spiritually and implement it—today!

LEVEL FIVE

LOVE

Speaks, Discovers, Acts, Encourages, and Serves

The wonderful story of Jim Conway's servanthood to his wife, Sally, is told in the winter 1993 issue of *Marriage Partnership:*

"*Jim:* 'When I was down, Sally carried me. Now when she's going through breast cancer, I'm carrying her. Marriage is made up of that kind of thing.'

"*Sally:* 'Jim's devotion to my recovery has been a model to everyone.'" Sally tells how Jim went through the biopsy, surgery, and days following. Then "'when I began chemotherapy and really lost my power, my dignity and my hair, he stood by me emotionally and physically. . . . He served me as if he had been hired to wait on my every need. I had an infection begin in my incision, and a large gaping hole developed. That had to be drained and dressed every day. My dear Jim would bend over me with his tender eyes, which were by that time getting a little dark-circled. He cared for that infection every day for nearly ten months.'

"To serve people means to wait on them, to minister to them, to attend to them. They are the ones having the five-course dinner and you are the waitress bringing it—only you will get no tip."[1]

Being a servant after saying "I do" is a greater challenge than before you get married. One couple we counseled struggled greatly with this. The wife, before marriage, couldn't do enough for her fiancé. She washed his clothes in college, jumped up to fill his empty glasses, and popped the popcorn while he lounged in front of the television.

A few days after this couple's honeymoon, the husband returned home from work to find breakfast and lunch dishes on the kitchen countertop, towels strewn around the bathroom, beds unmade, and nothing prepared for dinner.

Devasted, he felt unloved. He had married a servant to discover her tour of duty ended when she said, "I do."

Serving certainly isn't confined to wives. The Bible commands, "Let each of you regard one another as more important than himself" (Philippians 2:3, NASB). Myron expresses his love for me by traveling across town to run an errand, taking out the trash, vacuuming, clearing the table of dirty dishes, driving my mother to the doctor's office, accompanying me on weekend speaking engagements, emptying the dishwasher, grocery shopping, etc.

Since I resumed full-time writing at the same time Myron retired, I feel that he helps me more than I help him. But somewhere I read that if you ask a couple who helps the other more, both will name his or her spouse. It's a sign of a healthy, giving marriage.

True servanthood is sensing another's exhaustion or stress and stepping in to do unassigned chores. Servanthood is taking off your glasses to wear your spouse's and see life from his or her perspective; servanthood is stepping out of your shoes to discover how it feels to walk in your spouse's. Servanthood is a Christlike quality most essential to a magnificent marriage.

FOR STRONGER, DEEPER COUPLE LIFE

1. How much of a servant are you? Take time to rate yourself individually (keep your score to yourself). Give yourself 10 points each time your life matches one of the 10 described behaviors.
   - I'm happy to do the menial task, even if it's unpleasant.
   - I'm okay if my help goes unnoticed.
   - If my spouse doesn't help me, I continue to help my spouse.
   - I do not wait to be asked before helping.
   - I often let my spouse's body language tell me when I'm needed to pitch in and help. I don't wait for my spouse to scream, "I'm going to lose it" before I come to the rescue.
   - I love to surprise my spouse by doing one of his or her assigned chores before my spouse has a chance to do it.
   - I look on cleanup time in the garage or kitchen as a bonus time for interacting with my spouse.
   - I often ask my spouse how I can help.
   - I beg off helping only when mentally or physically exhausted.
   - I often ask God to make me a servant like Jesus.

2. How did you do? A score of 70–100 is super; 40–60, good; 20–30, fair.
3. Ask your husband or wife how you could improve as a helper.

Caution: The key is to refrain from all self-defense. Instead, thank your spouse for his or her input and take it to heart.

PUTTING SERVICE INTO PRACTICE

Whoever wants to become great among you must be your servant, and whoever wants to be first must be slave of all.

*For even the Son of Man did not come to be served, but to
serve, and to give his life as a ransom for many.*
MARK 10:43-45

Challenge for the Week: Ask Jesus to open your eyes and heart to a
specific way in which you could minister to your spouse.

TOGETHERNESS

Gazes, Makes Time, Plays, Converses, and **Bonds**

Today, when any couple seems the least bit intimate in their conversation, we may observe, "Oh! They're bonding!" Webster defines the word *bond* as "an adhesive, cementing material, or fusible ingredient that combines, unites, or strengthens."

We all want to be bonded with our spouse, fused together in a love that cannot be broken. But what adhesive will help us unite for a lifetime? Consider these:

1. *Be present.* Whatever the sacrifice, be there when the other speaks at a public gathering, appears in a drama, plays a sport, sings a solo, recites a poem, etc. The "power of presence" is felt even more when one has to cancel an activity to be present. As your eyes meet across the audience, you will feel the glue of love bonding you closer together.
2. *Ignore Keep Out signs.* When your spouse is miserable, feisty, fussy, or depressed, and you bypass the unpleasantness and enter that grouchy world to sit silently by a bedside, to touch

sympathetically, to hug, or to whisper an encouragement, your love is cemented. Even when the depressed spouse tells you to stay out, walk in, provided you are there only to be present in his or her sadness, not to give advice.

3. *Pray.* When your spouse is standing in one of life's many waiting lines (waiting to learn if he or she is being fired or hired, if a bid has been accepted by management, if a biopsy is negative, etc.), grab his or her hand and whisper a prayer, "Father, please let that phone ring with good news."

Prayer has a power to pull us together, to adhere us in a divine union. The bonding of prayer outweighs the stress of hearing one's self pray out loud a prayer of the heart.

4. *Go with the other.* One of you loves western music, and the other loves to hate it. One finds opera a delight, the other finds it a dread. One loves the stock car races, and the other can't tolerate the noise. But when you look your spouse in the eye and smile, saying, "I'm going with you tonight," the glue of togetherness welds you into oneness.

5. *Enter the other's world.* How caring when you think of a way to enter your spouse's workaday world to learn what his or her daily life is really like. Pride, sympathy, understanding, and caring can all be expressed in one visit to where the other works (if feasible).

6. *Read aloud.* A great way to bond before you go to sleep is to read a psalm from the Bible or, as Week 29 suggested, a chapter from Song of Songs.

7. *Return to your dating patterns.* Remember how happy you were together, whatever the activity? It didn't really matter if one of you loathed the opera or baseball. All you wanted to do was be together.

We might do well to focus more on our relationship, our times of companionship, the pure joy of being bonded together. Walter Wangerin, Jr., says, "There are three complete beings in a marriage—you, your spouse, and *the relationship* between you, which is . . . like a baby born from you both. It has its own character. . . . It comes cuddly and lovely, but very weak and in need of care and nourishment. . . . This living thing, this relationship . . . is your 'oneness.' . . . You are co-laborers committed to the care of a single (third!) life between you."[2]

FOR STRONGER, DEEPER COUPLE LIFE

1. Of the seven ways to bond, which three do you consider the most important? (You may also choose one of your own.) Why?
2. If both of you returned to your dating patterns, what would you like to do together? Discuss your responses.
3. What activity would you most enjoy doing with your spouse?

PUTTING BONDING INTO PRACTICE

"For this reason a man will leave his father and mother and be united to his wife, and the two will become one flesh." So they are no longer two, but one. Therefore what God has joined together, let man not separate.
MARK 10:7-9

Challenge for the Week: Plan to do an activity you once enjoyed together but have recently neglected.

ACCEPTANCE

Appreciates, Finds Good, Lets Go,
Stops Criticizing, and Honors

If Jesus Christ, the Lord of the universe, walked into our home, what would we do? We probably would stop whatever we were doing and run to greet him. Our spouse deserves the same welcome home. We honor and esteem one another by our eagerness to acknowledge our husband or wife as more important than our activities.

How time-conscious would we be? We certainly wouldn't check our watches, fidget, sigh, or rush away on another errand if Jesus were our guest. To honor another is to consider that person more important than the plans we have made or the things we want to do.

Gary Smalley summarizes his lack of honor for his wife, Norma, early in their marriage by writing, "I put a hundred things ahead of her. Work projects were more important to me than my mate, and while it's to my shame to admit it, there were countless times that a mountain trout, a small white golf ball, numerous church meetings, close friends and acquaintances—almost anything 'interesting' on television—took the place of honor which should have been reserved for Norma."[3]

What would our body language communicate? Our smiles would no doubt be as wide as our eyes as they gazed in love on Jesus. Our ears would act like antennae to pick up his every word.

More than half of honor is expressed in body language. For fifteen years I watched my upstairs neighbor, Linda, greet her husband, Bill. In rain, sleet, snow, or sunshine, when Bill left for work, Linda would hurry out on the balcony to wave good-bye. And when Bill returned, I would hear her call out "Hi, honey" from the top of the stairs, where she stood waiting.

A spirit of anticipation at our spouse's return communicates how highly we value him or her.

What would we say or avoid saying to Jesus? After welcoming him warmly we would most likely start listening, hanging on his every word. What he had to say would outweigh in importance what we wanted to add to the conversation. We definitely would not interrupt Jesus or finish his sentences for him. And as we listened, we would show respect for Jesus' words by not challenging, judging, or denying the truth of them.

Sad to report, we seldom demonstrate this level of respect for each other. Most often our lack of respect can be heard in our words. Here are four ways to disrespect our spouse when he or she speaks:

- *Correcting our spouse's perception of a problem.* In essence, we're saying to him or her, "You don't know what you're talking about."

    Spouse says: "Ellen is just too lazy. That's why she never finishes her homework on time."

    Other spouse responds: "That's the craziest idea! Where in the world did you come up with that! Ellen is far from lazy. Her schedule's too crowded, that's all."
- *Challenging our spouse's thinking on controversial issues, instead of displaying an interest in his or her perspective.*

Spouse says: "Tom was talking at work about all the healing value in vitamins, even in cancer prevention."

Other spouse responds: "That quack! Don't tell me anything he said. I don't want to hear."

• *Giving cliché answers to our spouse's problem.*

Spouse says: "The statistics scare me. I'm so worried Courtney might get pregnant in high school."

Other spouse responds: "It's obvious you're not trusting the Lord."

• *Shifting the conversation to ourselves or our interests before showing genuine interest in the subject introduced by our spouse.* Respect listens to understand, not to speak.

Spouse says: "Guess what? My boss is going to be a grandmother. Her daughter has tried for three years to get pregnant. The whole family is flying high."

Other spouse responds: "That's nice. Did you hear that Lou Ann and Bob are expecting in two months?"

Giving honor is the easiest skill to understand but one of the more difficult to achieve. To honor our spouse is to treat him or her as we would treat Jesus.

FOR STRONGER, DEEPER COUPLE LIFE

1. Do you honor your spouse with your
   • attention?
   • time?
   • spirit of anticipation?

If so, give an example. If not, which one of the three ways of honoring listed above is most difficult for you? Discuss your responses together.

2. Which one of the following disrespectful responses are you most likely to give? Why?
   • correcting spouse's perception of a problem

- challenging spouse's thinking on controversial issues
- giving cliché answers to spouse's problem
- shifting the conversation to yourself before showing genuine interest in the subject introduced by spouse

3. Individually write and share your "respectful response" to the following four sentences:
   a. *Spouse says:* "Ellen is just too lazy. That's why she never finishes her homework on time."
   Your response:
   b. *Spouse says:* "Tom was talking at work about all the healing value in vitamins, even in cancer prevention."
   Your response:
   c. *Spouse says:* "The statistics scare me. I'm so worried Courtney might get pregnant in high school."
   Your response:
   d. *Spouse says:* "Guess what? My boss is going to be a grandmother. Her daughter has tried for three years to get pregnant. The whole family is flying high."
   Your response:
   (Our suggested responses are at the bottom of the page.)

Answers:
a. "Somehow I've never thought of Ellen as lazy. Tell me why you think she is."
b. "There seems to be a lot written today about the medicinal value of vitamins and herbs."
c. "I don't like to admit it, but I worry about the same thing. I want to entrust her to the Lord, but I'm having problems."
d. "That's great! I'm glad she's so happy. She'll be a fun grandmother!"

4. Share your responses with your spouse. Rate each other's sentences on a scale of 1 to 5 (1 being disrespectful and 5 highly respectful).
5. Compare your answers with the authors' suggested responses on previous page.
6. Ask each other this question: Do you feel respected by me? If not, I would like to know why so I can stop doing or saying anything you find disrespectful.

PUTTING HONOR INTO PRACTICE

Honor one another above yourselves.
ROMANS 12:10

Challenge for the Week: Ask your spouse to tell you nicely, and in private, any times he or she feels a lack of respect from you in the future.

COMMITMENT

Wills, Teams Up, Gives, Disciplines, and Clings Tu

A̶s spouses, we must remember that family members were only invited to the wedding ceremony and reception to follow. We alone invited each other into our future.

Genesis 2:24 says, "A man will leave his father and mother and be united [cling to, attach himself] to his wife, and they will become one flesh." Ed Wheat comments, "God gave Adam two commands and one of them was to keep in-laws out of marriage. . . . An entirely new social unit is to be established."[4]

Each spouse must leave parents behind in order to place the other spouse before all other attachments; exit one dwelling to enter another; forsake all others to cling to or adhere together for a lifetime.

We never break the bond of love with our parents, but we do sever all ties of control. Breaking these ties sometimes feels like trying to untie a tangle in a delicate gold chain. We don't want to break the chain, but we must straighten out the entanglement. This is much easier said than done.

Myron and I cherish the memories of our favorite Christmas together, a Christmas that generated in-law disapproval and murmuring. We gave

185

up the traditional family gatherings for spending Christmas week in a remote, one-room mountain cabin with a potbellied stove for heat, a spring down the road for water, an outhouse at the back door for newspaper reading, and a classy mountain resort for skiing. The sheer joy of being together in an isolated mountain hollow made family disapproval easier to tolerate.

Choosing what's best for us will sometimes raise family members' eyebrows and objections. Such behaviors must inspire us to reach out and grab the other's hand as together we weather every storm of family disapproval.

Perhaps the following tips will help you in your relationship to your in-laws.

FIVE WAYS TO WIN YOUR IN-LAWS

1. Remember them with notes, special occasion cards, phone calls, and invitations to join you for dinner, a concert, etc.
2. Thank them for advice, even if unrequested. It never hurts to listen graciously, smile, thank them, and then forget the advice unless it's helpful to both spouses.
3. Request that they share their feelings about your proposed move, home purchase, church choice, job change, etc. After asking, use your best listening skills, listening for under-standing, not agreement. In-laws will feel less resentment toward your life change when you honor them with listening time. (Otherwise, you'll receive their resentment in small, ongoing pieces.)
4. Thank them by phone, by note, or in person for their union and nurture that provided your wonderful spouse!
5. Refrain from criticizing them, because your spouse may feel as if he or she is under attack. Work hard to find a kind word to say to your spouse about his/her parents.

FIVE FIRM STANDS TO TAKE

1. Accept only surprise gifts of money that come without strings attached. Parents sometimes lend money with a consuming interest in all your financial affairs.
2. Always speak highly of your spouse in front of family members, and don't allow them to criticize the one you love.
3. Seek counsel about all relationship problems together from a professional counselor, never from a family member or friend. Intimacy needs to be cloaked in privacy.
4. Decide never to side with your parents against your spouse.
5. Decorate and furnish your home together. Leave mothers, sisters, and all other family decorators behind when you shop for home furnishings. How your parents' home looks is not your model to follow.

FOR STRONGER, DEEPER COUPLE LIFE

Ask your spouse the following questions, and listen to understand, not to judge your spouse for his/her perceptions.

1. Do you feel you're number one in my life? If yes, what do I do to help you feel this way? If no, what would you like me to do in the future?
2. Do you feel I've left home (my parents) and made my family secondary to our life together? If not, what can I do to make us a priority in the future?
3. Are there ways in which you would like me to cling to you more tightly?
4. Which of the "Five Ways to Win Your In-Laws" could we carry out for better in-law relationships?
5. Which of the "Five Firm Stands to Take" should we take to keep our marriage in balance?

PUTTING COMMITMENT INTO PRACTICE

A man must leave his father and mother when
he marries so that he can be perfectly joined
to his wife, and the two shall be one.
EPHESIANS 5:31, TLB

Challenge for the Week: Contact your in-laws for no reason except to express your appreciation for their giving birth to and nurturing your wonderful spouse.

COMMUNICATION

Listens, Questions, Chooses, Cares, and Understands

Husband and wife communication will remain healthy only as long as you remember that emotions are neutral—not good or bad, not right or wrong.

Anger, for example, is not a bad emotion in and of itself. Anger may energize us to organize a community to fight against crime. In response to this same emotion, we might sin by calling people names, slamming doors, refusing to talk, or closing God out of our lives.

Once we accept the neutrality of emotions, we are ready to learn and practice *dialogue*. In *The Secret of Staying in Love,* John Powell labels *dialogue* as the sharing of emotions and feelings, as opposed to *discussion,* which he describes as the sharing of thoughts, values, ideas, plans, anything of a more intellectual nature. He insists that dialogue must precede decision making because "the static of unresolved and unexpressed emotions will block all attempt at the open, free flowing exchange that leads to plans, decisions, etc."[5] Dialogue is an essential skill to learn, because any "breakdown in human love and communication is always due to emotional problems."[6]

Holding different opinions does not block love unless one or both of us feel emotionally threatened by the other's opinion. According to Powell, dialogue is not intended to make us feel good. Sometimes it may even be difficult or painful. But if we want to be able to make plans without making war, dialogue is the key to open communication. Dialogue requires

- honesty when we want to protect ourselves by pretending or lying
- sharing emotions that we favor ignoring
- talking it out when we prefer pouting
- owning embarrassing feelings we would like to blame the other for causing
- talking about feelings when we prefer sticking to facts

Is dialogue worth the effort? Yes! Because our emotions are like our fingerprints or DNA—uniquely ours—how can we know each other unless, now and then, we reach down inside and pull out an emotion to share?

When a spouse admits, "I feel like a duck out of water when I visit your parents. Everything is fragile and costly, and I'm big and clumsy," how would we respond to that admission of true feelings? Would we

- *insist the other's feelings are somehow wrong?* "You know Mom and Dad love you, and their house is always open."
- *try to make the sharing spouse feel guilty for his or her emotions?* "You're impossible! How will you ever get along with Mom and Dad with feelings like that?"
- *judge or criticize the feelings?* Saying, "That's the craziest thing you've ever said!" implies that the owner of such emotions is somehow flawed.

- *accept your spouse's feeling?* "You must have a really hard time when I want to visit Mom and Dad for longer than an hour."

Dialogue is for understanding only, not to produce a winner or reach a decision. When engaging in dialogue, we may even need to place a hand over our mouth to keep from interrupting, correcting, or questioning too frequently. If we think we accurately understand our spouse's dialogue, we make what we've previously labeled as a "perception check"—a question that reflects back to the speaker what the listener thinks has been said and in essence asks, "Have I heard you correctly?"

FOR STRONGER, DEEPER COUPLE LIFE

1. Choose one of you to be the "listening spouse" and the other to be the "talking spouse." Set a timer (if available) for three minutes.
2. The "talking spouse" chooses an ongoing argument (maybe about visiting a certain family member, money, sex, work division in the house, buying a new car instead of new draperies, child discipline, etc.). He/she talks for three minutes, sharing, "I feel [emotion] when you [name of problem] because [reason for emotional response]."
   Caution: Although the "listening spouse" remains silent, he/she is still involved with good body language: leaning forward, nodding, focusing eyes, keeping face frown-free and pleasant, etc.
3. When the buzzer sounds, the listening spouse makes a first perception check: "It sounds to me as if you feel _____ when I _____ because _____."
4. If the speaker feels misunderstood, continue the dialogue until the speaker accepts the listener's perception as correct. Then reverse roles and do the exercise again!
5. Spend time together, if possible, after the exercise. Take a long

walk holding hands or stretch out on the bed with soft, background music playing. Caress and stroke gently until all stirred emotions subside.

PUTTING UNDERSTANDING INTO PRACTICE

We will lovingly follow the truth at all times—speaking truly, dealing truly, living truly—and so become more and more in every way like Christ.
EPHESIANS 4:15-16, TLB

Challenge for the Week: Set a time for the listener to share his or her feelings about the problem the other raised. Follow all of the above instructions for dialoguing.

Then hold a decision-making session. Begin that time with each spouse making a perception check to see if the other's emotions are understood. Explore options and attempt reaching agreement with a compromise. (You may want to refer to the skills on how to choose a church. See Week 30.) Whenever you fail to reach a decision, take a rest and talk again.

CONFLICT RESOLUTION

Chooses, Focuses, Replaces, Requires, and Surrenders

Two paths diverged in a wood, and I—
I took the one less traveled by,
And that has made all the difference.
—Robert Frost, "The Road Not Taken"

Remember the only two possible responses to conflict? Either we choose to draw within and protect ourselves from pain, or we choose to reach out and gain understanding of our spouse and ourselves.

Surrendering our weapons of self-defense feels somewhat like getting caught naked in the living room by unexpected guests. But in order to grow in intimacy as a couple, we need to work at letting go of our self-protection.

Self-protection is a way of relating to one another while trying to protect ourselves from pain, sadness, insecurity, fear, disappointment, and discomfort. It is a manipulative way of interacting with others to "manage" their behavior so it won't threaten us.

We may ask, "Isn't it just common sense to protect ourselves from disturbing, uncomfortable feelings and pain?" The problem is we cannot be open and self-protecting at the same time. In protecting ourselves we

- shut off love
- refuse to take responsibility for our own feelings and actions: "You make me angry!" If I play the blame game, I keep the focus on you and manage to protect myself from unpleasant feelings.
- avoid answering questions that reveal more than we want to reveal, thus settling for lying instead of speaking the truth in love
- focus on proving our partner wrong with threats, silent treatment, violent bursts of anger, accusations, crying bouts, criticism, complaining, sarcasm, lying, or lecturing

Christian author Larry Crabb says, "The mark of maturity is love, and the essence of love is relating without self-protection" because it "stains our best efforts to love, shaping our style of relating to fit defensive purposes. Much of our polite conversation and pleasant fellowship is little more than two protective styles of relating that comfortably mesh. . . . Our insulating layers of friendliness and appropriate involvement work to keep us from touching the terrible pain of previously felt disappointment. We have all been let down, and it hurt. Our commitment is to never hurt like that again. We therefore try to love from a distance. But it can't be done."[7]

Consider the patterns of this self-protecting couple: The wife longs to be appreciated. She loses herself in performing to please. She is engrossed in church ministry. Her friends are often those she counsels. This is her protection against being rejected. She feels comfortable only if she knows people need her. She rarely sits still. If she watches television, she knits. Her busyness is a defense against intimate relationships. Her husband is a quiet, gentle man who praises his wife. He, too, distances himself from meaningful relationships by remaining aloof and without close friends. His fear of failure is protected by his quiet, distant mode. His fear of failure sometimes affects his lovemaking. He finds emotional safety in books and newspapers. He has difficulty making direct requests. Can you see where this couple must surrender their weapons of self-defense in order to be vulnerable to one another?

This couple was us ten years ago. But because we longed for intimacy, we are slowly letting down our defenses. We determined to choose the path less traveled, the path of understanding and learning about each other and ourselves.

FOR STRONGER, DEEPER COUPLE LIFE

1. For this exercise, write individually for five minutes, answering the following questions/statements:
   - In what ways do you protect yourself?
   - What insecurities lead you to self-protect?
   - Identify self-protections you feel safe in revealing.
   - Name self-protections you would like to overcome.

2. Now switch papers with your spouse. After you have read your spouse's description, first thank your spouse for trusting you enough to reveal himself or herself. If you want to ask a question about what your spouse has written, make sure it is a judgment-free question that is asked for one reason only: so that you may more greatly understand the one you love.

PUTTING CONFLICT RESOLUTION INTO PRACTICE

Love is patient, love is kind. It does not envy, it does not
boast, it is not proud. It is not rude, it is not self-seeking, it
is not easily angered, it keeps no record of wrongs. Love

does not delight in evil but rejoices with the truth. It always protects, always trusts, always hopes, always perseveres.
1 CORINTHIANS 13:4-7

Challenge for the Week: Surrender your weapons of self-defense. Sound difficult? It is. By ourselves we often can't even name our efforts at self-protection. But God searches the heart. Ask him to reveal any self-protection to you.

FORGIVENESS

Touches, Resolves, Restores, Absolves, and Graces

Forgiveness is a four-way stop sign where spouses meet and yield in humility to each other. One confesses, "I need you to forgive me"; the other absolves the offending spouse of guilt with the reassuring words "I forgive you."

But to forgive is never easy. Forgiveness is a process, an inner work of God's grace.

When we have said "I forgive you" to our spouse, we are often surprised to discover anger lingering in our heart. In the courtroom of our mind we've remained seated in the judge's chair, still pronouncing the same sentence: "Guilty of first-degree insult to my ego."

At moments like this we can do nothing but call out to God, "I'm helpless. You'll have to forgive for me. I lack sufficient grace."

The apostle Peter, who had an ongoing battle with foot-in-the-mouth disease, addresses our problem with the command to "grow in the grace and knowledge of our Lord and Savior Jesus Christ" (2 Peter 3:18). This verse reminds us of two truths:

- Grace is a growth process, not a once-and-for-all experience.
- Grace is not something we feel, but something we receive from God that enables us to forgive our spouse.

In the Bible, grace is giving love to the unlovable, forgiveness to the unforgiving, mercy to the unmerciful. In other words, grace is forgiving the other when he or she least deserves it, just as Jesus Christ graces us with forgiveness and eternal life that we could never earn or deserve. Someone has said that "anything more than hell is more than we deserve."

The true story of Shamel, a nineteenth-century Russian, may help us understand God's awesome generosity toward sinners.

Shamel led a guerilla band who fought against the oppressive czarist regime. With his fighting men were women, children, and livestock—a little interdependent universe whose survival depended on mutual trust and support.

Then one day stealing broke out in the camp.

Shamel laid down the law "Thou shalt not steal" and attached a penalty, "Anyone caught stealing would publicly receive one hundred lashes." One day the thief was caught and brought before Shamel for judgment.

The thief was his mother.

Shamel faced anarchy if moral law was not enforced in his small universe. But to lash his mother was unthinkable. Shamel wrestled three days and nights before he emerged from his tent and announced his decision: "The law must stand. The penalty must be paid. I will receive the one hundred lashes for my mother."

Just as Shamel's lashing disclosed the horror of his mother's sin and the cost of her son's forgiveness, the Cross of Christ discloses the horror of my sin and the cost of God's forgiveness.

When we refuse to forgive, we crucify Christ afresh and harden our hearts, ignoring the price he paid to forgive us.

Only in understanding his grace will we grace one another with forgiveness.

FOR STRONGER, DEEPER COUPLE LIFE

1. Read the following Scripture passages aloud.

He does not treat us as our sins deserve
or repay us according to our iniquities.
PSALM 103:10

As far as the east is from the west, so far has
he removed our transgressions from us.
PSALM 103:12

Be kind to each other, tenderhearted, forgiving one another,
just as God has forgiven you because you belong to Christ.
EPHESIANS 4:32, TLB

Bear with each other and forgive whatever
grievances you may have against one another.
Forgive as the Lord forgave you.
COLOSSIANS 3:13

2. How do you feel when you think of Christ taking your place on the cross to die so that you may be forgiven?
3. Grace is *God's Riches At Christ's Expense*. We receive the riches of forgiveness because of what Christ did for us on the cross, not because of what we did. Does it make sense to you to leap from the truth of the Cross to the truth that forgiveness is never optional for a Christian? If not, why not?

4. End this time by reading aloud the prayer provided below.

PUTTING GRACE INTO PRACTICE

*For it is by grace you have been saved, through
faith—and this not from yourselves, it is the gift of
God—not by works, so that no one can boast.*
EPHESIANS 2:8-9

Challenge for the Week: Pray daily, "Father, please fill my heart with your grace so I'll have the grace to forgive my spouse whenever I need it. Amen."

EMOTIONAL INTIMACY

Opens Up, Speaks Candidly, Hugs, Empathizes, and Trusts

Proverbs 31 paints a bold and beautiful picture of a wife trusted by her husband: "If you can find a truly good wife, she is worth more than precious gems! Her husband can trust her, and she will richly satisfy his needs. She will . . . help him all her life. When she speaks, her words are wise, and kindness is the rule for everything she says" (Proverbs 31: 10-12, 26, TLB). "The heart of her husband trusts in her confidently and relies on and believes in her safely" (Proverbs 31:11, AMP). What does this passage have to say to both husbands and wives?

First, that *a trusted spouse richly satisfies his or her lover's needs (verse 11).* All of us would hurry home to a spouse who richly satisfied our need to feel we belong, our need to feel respected, our need to receive caring kindness, tender affection, loving words, and deep intimacy. Our heart could quickly find a home in the heart of a spouse like this.

Second, *a trusted spouse will help his or her spouse as long as they live (verse 12).* John Powell says, "In practice, love implies that I am ready and willing to forego my own convenience, to invest my own time, and even to risk my own security to promote your satisfaction, security and development."[8] Trust thrives with a spouse as devoted as this!

Third, *before he or she ever speaks, a trusted spouse asks, "Is this the kind thing to say?" (verse 26).* If we know our spouse's every word will be kind, we are set free to trust him or her. Total trust is a deep, warm sense of belonging to the other, knowing without a doubt that our spouse is for us and not against us. Trust frees us to live open, transparent, vulnerable lives together, and trust enables us to vow the following without fear:

> *My darling,*
> *I will trust God to direct and change you.*
> *I will make it my priority to meet your needs.*
> *I will empathize with and help heal your hurts.*
> *I will share the truth of my needs with you in love.*
> *I will share the truth of my hurts with you in love.*
> *I will treat the truth you share with me confidentially, as our*
> *truth.*[9]

William L. Coleman provides us with three quick reasons a husband may trust his wife:

- She does not shrug off his problems.
- She cares enough to try to understand.
- She will accept what she cannot understand.[10]

What must we be able to trust about our spouse in order for emotional intimacy to develop and grow? Here are six things we must know:

1. I can come to you and share my feelings without being criticized.
2. I can trust you with my honesty. You won't belittle me, ignore me, dismiss me, or put me down.

3. You understand the subject of emotions so that, when I share my feelings, you will not feel too threatened to cope.
4. You accept me as I am with my strengths and weaknesses. I do not have to change in order for you to accept me.
5. I will be able to accept my emotions as God's good gift to enrich my life. I must not deny them or suppress them but learn to express them in a way that honors God and sets me free of their dominion.
6. When you share feelings, you are only looking for my understanding and acceptance, never trying to manipulate me to act a certain way.

FOR STRONGER, DEEPER COUPLE LIFE

Take turns asking each other the following questions:

1. How do I do in satisfying your needs? in being a real helper to you? in speaking only kind words?
2. How do you feel about our taking the vow on the previous page? Which one of the six "I will" statements would you find most difficult?
3. Would the three reasons listed by William Coleman be sufficient for you to open up to me with your private thoughts and secret emotions? If not, what else would you need from me?
4. Which of the six things we must know, if any, do you feel you really don't know for sure about me? What could I do to increase that trust?

Her husband [his wife] can trust her [him], and she [he]
will richly satisfy his [her] needs.
PROVERBS 31:11, TLB

Challenge for the Week: This lesson, one of the most important in this book, offers short and longer lists of the ingredients of emotional trust in a marriage. Choose the list that challenges you the most, study it daily, and talk to your spouse about it at dinner or bedtime one night this week.

PHYSICAL INTIMACY

Strokes, Romances, Excites, Communicates,
and Ministers

As Christians we must beware of the *Playboy* mentality in secular movies, plays, and novels that idealizes sexual manipulation and its philosophy that sex is nothing more than a fun thing to do. Do it with any available body, do it as often as you can, and do it any way you like it. Satisfy me—now! That's what "fun sex" is all about!

One problem is that what's fun for one may prove to be agony for another. A manipulative husband may demand that his wife perform sex in a way that is disliked by her, that she lose weight so her body will be more pleasing to his eyes, or that she stop her complaining and give him sex as often as he needs it.

A manipulative wife may promise more sex for less golf. When asked about sex, she may immediately attack her husband's lack of romanticism to take the spotlight off her reluctance; she may use exhaustion as an excuse for no sex and also as a way of suggesting that if her husband paid for maid service she would be more ready for sex.

To manipulate to get what we want is a shortcut to emptiness. After using another human being for our satisfaction, the good feeling of sex doesn't last long: "We try to manipulate people into loving us. We know our loneliness can be relieved by the love of others. We know we must feel loved. The paradox is this: *If we seek to fill the void, we will find no relief but only a deeper vacuum.*"[11]

And what happens when our manipulation fails? Manipulation functions as a one-way street to frustration and anger. But there is another choice.

If manipulative sex leaves us frustrated and angry, the only other option, according to author Larry Crabb, is to "shift from manipulating your spouse to meet your needs to ministering to your spouse's needs."[12]

The opposite of manipulating a body is ministering to a person during sex—being aware not only of your spouse's body, but also of his or her spirit and soul. Ministry insists, "I'll be satisfied sexually only when I satisfy you."

The act of marriage is like the service of love, asking not what can I get from you, but how best may I experience with you the beautiful passion, intimacy, and delight of married oneness?

If each of us has the goal of ministering to the other, then we will be satisfied sexually only when the other is satisfied in his or her soul as well as body.

FOR STRONGER, DEEPER COUPLE LIFE

1. Take turns asking each other the following questions. They may open new avenues of understanding in your sexual relationship.
   • Do resentment, anxiety, or guilt ever block your sexual joy? Explain.
   • Do you ever feel manipulated by me in order to fulfill my sexual desires? If so, please explain.

Caution: The "listening spouse" must remember that feelings, not facts, are being shared. This is not a time to criticize your spouse.

2. Discuss together how you could adopt a goal of ministering to each other's sexual needs instead of thinking of your own.
3. Do the following exercise individually: If you could plan a perfectly wonderful evening of sexual intimacy with your spouse, what ten things would you include? List on paper ten details about how you would like to be romanced, preparation for lovemaking by you and your spouse, attire, if any, fragrances, foreplay, time, place, positions, after-time, etc.
4. You have just created your very own sex map! Share it with your spouse and encourage him/her to ask questions. Swap maps, so each of you has a reminder of what the other finds pleasurable.

Caution: Remember not to use your sex map to manipulate!

PUTTING PHYSICAL INTIMACY INTO PRACTICE

Each of you should look not only to your own
interests, but also to the interests of others.
PHILIPPIANS 2:4

Challenge for the Week: Think and pray about shifting your goals from self-fulfillment to fulfilling your spouse's needs.

SPIRITUAL LIFE
Blesses, Reaches, Locates, Grows, and **Enthrones**

W hen a thousand people were asked, "What makes a marriage last?" two answers practically tied for first place: (1) They love each other; (2) They have a faith in God.[13]

What is "faith in God"? Two questions help us find the answer for ourselves:

1. If you were to die tonight, do you know for sure you would go to heaven? (There are only two possible answers: yes and no.) Please choose your answer before reading question 2.

2. If you were to die tonight and go to heaven and God asked you, "Why should I let you into heaven?" what would you say? Stop and write your individual answers here:

Wife: _____

_____

Husband: _____

_____

God intends for us to know that we have eternal life. In 1 John 5:13, the apostle reveals why he wrote this book: "I write these things to you who believe in the name of the Son of God so that you may know that you have eternal life."

Individually we need to come to the place where we can say, "Yes! I know I'm going to heaven."

Any answer to question 2 that does not include faith in Jesus Christ points to a lack of saving faith. If we say, "I'm a good person"; "I've gone to church all my life"; "I've kept the Ten Commandments"; etc., our answers reveal that we are depending on ourselves and what we have done to open the door into heaven for us. If we believe Christ died in our place on Calvary, we trust his work, not ours.

Suppose you are facing an incredibly deep canyon that is one hundred feet wide. Imagine every man, woman, and child that has ever lived or ever will live on earth lined up on one side of the canyon. They have to make it to the other side to receive eternal life. If they don't make it, they're lost. They think they have to jump. The world record in the broad jump is nearly thirty-one feet.

How many people in the whole human race can jump the hundred-foot-wide canyon? None!

Some may jump farther than others, but none would come close to making it. All would fall short. This is precisely how it is spiritually. The distance between God and man is the distance between perfection and imperfection, holiness and sinfulness, life and death.

Many people exhaust themselves trying to jump the canyon. All the religions, philosophies, and moral systems are essentially books of instruction on how to become a better jumper. But our basic problem is not having the *power* to live as we know we ought. None of us is good enough to jump across the canyon. We are all doomed to spiritual death— separation from God.

But the gospel—the Good News—is that in Christ, God has done for us what we could not do for ourselves. He has bridged the gap with his cross. Why should we be so foolish as to try to jump, when we can walk across the bridge of Calvary to eternity?

"For the wages of sin is death, but the gift of God is eternal life in Christ Jesus our Lord" (Romans 6:23). That's the gospel, the Good News of the Christian faith: God offers heaven to us as a free gift because it has been paid for by Christ.

FOR STRONGER, DEEPER COUPLE LIFE

Share together your responses to the following questions:

1. Have you ever invited Christ into your life?
2. What thoughts do you have when asked this question?
3. What emotions do you feel?
4. Does the gospel make sense to you? If so, why? If not, in what ways doesn't it make sense?

We receive eternal life by receiving Jesus Christ himself. He is both the Gift and the Giver; we can't have the one without the other.[14]

PUTTING OUR SPIRITUAL LIFE INTO PRACTICE

Here I am! I stand at the door and knock. If anyone hears
my voice and opens the door, I will come in and eat with
him, and he with me.
REVELATION 3:20

Challenge for the Week: Think seriously about Christ's call on your life, and pray this simple prayer: "Lord Jesus, I choose to stop trusting in myself and start trusting in you and in what you accomplished when you

211

died in my place on the cross. I know that I am a sinner, and I turn from my sins and ask your forgiveness. I invite you to come and live inside me. I want you to be number one in my life. I totally commit myself to learning your will and obeying it the rest of my life. Thank you, Jesus. Amen."

LEVEL ONE

1. Hal Larson, *If He Loves Me, Why Doesn't He Tell Me?* (San Franciso: Halo Books, 1994).
2. Ed Wheat, *Love Life for Every Married Couple* (Grand Rapids: Zondervan, 1980), 92.
3. Cecil B. Murphey, *Devotions for Lovers* (Old Tappan, N.J.: Revell, 1982), 44.
4. H. Norman Wright, *Homemade* 14, no. 11 (November 1990).
5. John and Linda Friel, "The Little Things in Life," *Changes* (October 1993): 15.
6. Diane Ackerman, "Are You Made for Love?" *Parade* (June 19, 1994): 8.
7. James Dobson, *Focus on the Family Bulletin* 3, no. 9 (October 1990).
8. Ackerman, "Are You Made for Love?" 8.
9. Charles Swindoll, *Homemade* 15, no. 1 (January 1991).
10. Harvey Mackay, "Listen Up!" *Successful Meetings* (July 1993).
11. Fay Bustanoby and Andre Bustanoby, *Just Talk to Me* (Grand Rapids: Zondervan, 1981), 56.
12. O. Dean Martin, *Good Marriages Don't Just Happen, You Make Them Happen* (Old Tappan, N.J.: Revell, 1984), 100.
13. Dr. John Paul and Dr. Margaret Paul, *Do I Have to Give Up Me to Be Loved by You?* (Minneapolis: CompCare Publishers, 1983), 6.
14. Murphey, *Devotions for Lovers,* 68.
15. William L. Coleman, *What Makes a Marriage Last?* (San Bernardino, Calif.: Here's Life Publishers, 1990), 57.
16. Jay Kesler, "Q & A," *Marriage Partnership* (winter 1993): 67.

17. Dr. Virgil Satir, *Homemade* 14, no. 6 (June 1990).
18. Gary Chapman, *Five Love Languages* (Chicago: Northfield Publishing, 1992), 105.
19. Murphey, *Devotions for Lovers,* 41–42.
20. Marianne K. Hering, "Believe Well, Live Well," *Family Policy Newsletter* (May 1994), as reported in *Focus on the Family* (September 1994).
21. Larson Mayo and Mary Ann Mayo, quoted in Hering, "Believe Well, Live Well," 4.
22. Ibid.
23. Louis H. Evans, *Your Marriage: Duel or Duet* (Old Tappan, N.J.: Revell, 1974), 99.

LEVEL TWO

1. Willard F. Harley, Jr., *His Needs, Her Needs: Building an Affair-Proof Marriage* (Grand Rapids: Revell, 1986), 10.
2. Chapman, *Five Love Languages,* 39–116.
3. Kesler, "Q & A."
4. J. Allan Petersen, *Homemade* 15, no. 12 (December 1991).
5. James Dobson, *Focus on the Family Bulletin* 3, no. 9 (October 1990), as first told by Dr. Dobson in *Straight Talk to Men and Their Wives.* A story by Dr. Richard Seizer.
6. Harley, *His Needs, Her Needs,* 58, 65.
7. Paul Tournier, *To Understand Each Other* (Richmond, Va.: John Knox Press, 1967), 29.
8. J. Allan Petersen, *Homemade* 16, no. 7 (July 1991).
9. John Powell, *Why Am I Afraid to Tell You Who I Am?* (Niles, Ill.: Argus Communications, 1969), 155.
10. Ann Landers, *Richmond Times Dispatch,* 4 October 1994.
11. Gary Smalley with John Trent, *Love Is a Decision* (New York: Pocket Books, Simon & Schuster, Inc., 1989), 167.
12. C. S. Lewis, *A Grief Observed* (New York: The Seabury Press, Inc., 1961), 6–7.

13. Sheldon Vanauken, *A Severe Mercy* (New York: Harper & Row, 1977), 36.
14. Lawrence J. Crabb, Jr., *The Marriage Builder* (Grand Rapids: Zondervan, 1982), 29.
15. Ibid., 30.

LEVEL THREE

1. J. Allan Petersen, *Homemade* 14, no. 4 (May 1990).
2. Ann Landers, *Richmond Times Dispatch,* 25 October 1994.
3. Lois Leiderman Davitz, "Why Men Divorce," *McCall's,* March 1987, 26.
4. Carole Mayhall, "Gifts You Can Give Your Marriage," *Today's Christian Woman,* November/December 1993, 81.
5. Harley, *His Needs, Her Needs,* 81–82.
6. Tim LaHaye, *How to Be Happy Though Married* (Wheaton, Ill.: Tyndale, 1968), 101.
7. Walter Wangerin, Jr., *As for Me and My House* (Nashville: Nelson, 1990), 245–46.
8. Ibid., 246–47.
9. Fay Bustanoby and A. Bustanoby, *Just Talk to Me,* 74.
10. David Hocking and Carole Hocking, *Romantic Lovers* (Eugene, Oreg.: Harvest House, 1982), 6.
11. Ibid., 154–57.
12. Coleman, *What Makes a Marriage Last?* 98.

LEVEL FOUR

1. Paul Lee Tan, *Encyclopedia of 7700 Illustrations* (Chicago: R. R. Donnelley and Sons, Inc., 1979), 338.
2. Gayle Roper, *Who Cares? Cultivating the Fine Art of Loving One Another* (Wheaton, Ill.: Harold Shaw Publishers, 1992), 83.
3. Smalley with Trent, *Love Is a Decision,* 133.
4. Alice Chapin, *400 Creative Ways to Say I Love You* (Wheaton, Ill.: Tyndale, 1981), 96–97.

5. Wheat, *Love Life*, 127.
6. Gary Smalley, *The Joy of Committed Love* (Grand Rapids: Zondervan, 1982), 224.
7. John Drescher, *Homemade* 14, no. 4 (April 1990).
8. Dietrich Bonhoeffer, *Life Together* (New York: Harper & Row, 1954), 112.
9. Judy Markey, "The Secret Life of the American Wife," *Woman's Day*, 29 May 1991, 41.
10. Alice Fryling and Robert Fryling, *A Handbook for Married Couples* (Downers Grove, Ill.: InterVarsity Press, 1984), 81.
11. Dean Ornish, M.D., *Stress, Diet and Your Heart* (New York: Holt, Rinehart & Winston, 1982), 33.
12. John Powell, *The Secret of Staying in Love* (Niles, Ill.: Argus Communications, 1974), 78–79.
13. H. Norman Wright, *Communication: Key to Your Marriage* (Glendale, Calif.: G/L Publications, 1974), 165.
14. Cliff Penner and Joyce Penner, "The Best Time to Talk about Sex," *Marriage Partnership* (summer 1992).
15. Wangerin, *As for Me*, 190–91.
16. C. Penner and J. Penner, "The Best Time," 76.
17. Wangerin, *As for Me*, 189.
18. James C. Dobson, *Love for a Lifetime* (Sisters, Oreg.: Multnomah Books, 1993), 65.
19. Wheat, *Love Life*, 69.
20. Dr. Willard F. Harley, Jr., *Love Busters* (Grand Rapids: Revell, 1992), 85.
21. Chapman, *Five Love Languages*, 121.
22. John Powell, *Why Am I Afraid to Love?* (Niles, Ill.: Argus Communications, 1972), 126.
23. Larry Dossey, M.D., *Healing Words: The Power of Prayer and the Practice of Medicine*, quoted in Hering, "Believe Well, Live Well."

LEVEL FIVE

1. Roper, *Who Cares?* 60.
2. Wangerin, *As for Me,* 45–46.
3. Smalley with Trent, *Love Is a Decision,* 25.
4. Wheat, *Love Life,* 144.
5. Powell, *Staying in Love,* 75.
6. Ibid., 73.
7. Larry Crabb, Jr., *Inside Out* (Colorado Springs: NavPress, 1988), 128, 99.
8. Powell, *Staying in Love,* 44.
9. David Ferguson et al., *The Pursuit of Intimacy* (Nashville: Nelson, 1993), 190.
10. Coleman, *What Makes a Marriage Last?* 94.
11. Powell, *Why Am I Afraid to Love?* 83.
12. Crabb, *The Marriage Builder,* 97.
13. Coleman, *What Makes a Marriage Last?* 83.
14. Special thanks for the material in this lesson to Dr. Earl Morey, former pastor, St. Giles' Presbyterian Church in Richmond, Virginia, for his "Share Your Faith," which used material from James Kennedy's *Evangelism Explosion.*

CHART A:
THE TOP TEN AREAS OF COUPLE LIFE: A CUMULATIVE CHART

AREAS	LEVEL 1	LEVEL 2	LEVEL 3	LEVEL 4	LEVEL 5
Love	Speaks	Discovers	Acts	Encourages	Serves
Togetherness	Gazes	Makes Time	Plays	Converses	Bonds
Acceptance	Appreciates	Finds Good	Lets Go	Stops Criticizing	Honors
Commitment	Wills	Teams Up	Gives	Disciplines	Clings To
Communication	Listens	Questions	Chooses	Cares	Understands
Conflict Resolution	Chooses	Focuses	Replaces	Requires	Surrenders
Forgiveness	Touches	Resolves	Restores	Absolves	Graces
Emotional Intimacy	Opens Up	Speaks Candidly	Hugs	Empathizes	Trusts
Physical Intimacy	Strokes	Romances	Excites	Communicates	Ministers
Spiritual Life	Blesses	Reaches	Locates	Grows	Enthrones

Chart B: Ledger for Couples

Lesson	Date Completed	Wife's Initials	Husband's Initials
LEVEL ONE			
Week 1: Love *Speaks*	10/26	Rmm	Brow
Week 2: Togetherness *Gazes*			
Week 3: Acceptance *Appreciates*			
Week 4: Commitment *Wills*			
Week 5: Communication *Listens*			
Week 6: Conflict Resolution *Chooses*			
Week 7: Forgiveness *Touches*			
Week 8: Emotional Intimacy *Opens Up*			
Week 9: Physical Intimacy *Strokes*			
Week 10: Spiritual Life *Blesses*			
LEVEL TWO			
Week 11: Love *Discovers*			
Week 12: Togetherness *Makes Time*			
Week 13: Acceptance *Finds Good*			
Week 14: Commitment *Teams Up*			
Week 15: Communication *Questions*			
Week 16: Conflict Resolution *Focuses*			
Week 17: Forgiveness *Resolves*			
Week 18: Emotional Intimacy *Speaks Candidly*			
Week 19: Physical Intimacy *Romances*			
Week 20: Spiritual Life *Reaches*			

CHART B: LEDGER FOR COUPLES

Lesson	Date Completed	Wife's Initials	Husband's Initials
LEVEL THREE			
Week 21: Love *Acts*	_____	_____	_____
Week 22: Togetherness *Plays*	_____	_____	_____
Week 23: Acceptance *Lets Go*	_____	_____	_____
Week 24: Commitment *Gives*	_____	_____	_____
Week 25: Communication *Chooses*	_____	_____	_____
Week 26: Conflict Resolution *Replaces*	_____	_____	_____
Week 27: Forgiveness *Restores*	_____	_____	_____
Week 28: Emotional Intimacy *Hugs*	_____	_____	_____
Week 29: Physical Intimacy *Excites*	_____	_____	_____
Week 30: Spiritual Life *Locates*	_____	_____	_____
LEVEL FOUR			
Week 31: Love *Encourages*	_____	_____	_____
Week 32: Togetherness *Converses*	_____	_____	_____
Week 33: Acceptance *Stops Criticizing*	_____	_____	_____
Week 34: Commitment *Disciplines*	_____	_____	_____
Week 35: Communication *Cares*	_____	_____	_____
Week 36: Conflict Resolution *Requires*	_____	_____	_____
Week 37: Forgiveness *Absolves*	_____	_____	_____
Week 38: Emotional Intimacy *Empathizes*	_____	_____	_____
Week 39: Physical Intimacy *Communicates*	_____	_____	_____
Week 40: Spiritual Life *Grows*	_____	_____	_____

CHART B: LEDGER FOR COUPLES

Lesson	Date Completed	Wife's Initials	Husband's Initials
Week 41: Love *Serves*	_____	_____	_____
Week 42: Togetherness *Bonds*	_____	_____	_____
Week 43: Acceptance *Honors*	_____	_____	_____
Week 44: Commitment *Clings To*	_____	_____	_____
Week 45: Communication *Understands*	_____	_____	_____
Week 46: Conflict Resolution *Surrenders*	_____	_____	_____
Week 47: Forgiveness *Graces*	_____	_____	_____
Week 48: Emotional Intimacy *Trusts*	_____	_____	_____
Week 49: Physical Intimacy *Ministers*	_____	_____	_____
Week 50: Spiritual Life *Enthrones*	_____	_____	_____

LEVEL FIVE